"The story of the woman at the well [is full of] jewels, and Chris Anderson helps us s[ee] [grace] and hope for sinners. This book draws us into the conversation beside the well to see ourselves and, above all, to see the Hero of the story. Jesus' stunning love and thirst-quenching grace is enough to cause us, like the Samaritan woman, to leave our stuff and run around the corner or around the world to tell others of Christ, 'the Savior of the world'!"

Tim Keesee—Executive Director, Frontline Missions International; author of *Dispatches from the Front: Stories of Gospel Advance in the World's Difficult Places*

"In this little book, *The God Who Satisfies*, a gifted poet transitions to prose. I have known Chris Anderson for over two decades, first as a student and then as a fellow laborer in the work of the Kingdom. This book's focus on the Samaritan woman is full of Christ and the glorious gospel of grace. Written in an easy-to-read, popular style full of real-life illustrations, the book effectively links helpful background facts and precisely-stated theological truths to experiential application. Throughout, the heart of the author is exposed. What Mr. Anderson writes is not just theory, but the expression of his own experience with the all-sufficient Savior. It is a book that can be used for evangelism as well as for warming the believer's heart to renewed gratitude for what Christ has abundantly supplied."

Michael P. V. Barrett—Academic Dean & Professor, Puritan Reformed Theological Seminary; author of *Complete in Him, Beginning at Moses,* and other books

"Over the space of His earthly ministry, Jesus must have had hundreds of personal conversations with people, yet the number of them recorded in Scripture is actually quite limited. So, the dialogues God wrote down for us are rich with truth about Jesus, His mission, and the people He came to save. Chris Anderson mines the riches of John 4 and in *The God Who Satisfies* paints a beautiful, compelling portrait that shows us God's glory in the face of Jesus Christ (2 Corinthians 4:6). Read it to grow in your love for Jesus Christ. Read it to marvel at His mercy toward sinners—like us. Read it to learn from the Master how to point them to the God Who satisfies!"

Dave Doran—Pastor, Inter-City Baptist Church, Allen Park, MI; President, Detroit Baptist Theological Seminary

THE GOD WHO
SATISFIES

How Jesus Seeks, Saves, and Satisfies
Samaritan Women—*Like Us*

CHRIS ANDERSON

Copy Editor: Abby Huffstutler
Book Design: Jared & Holly Miller (keskillc.com)
Art Director: Joe Tyrpak

First printing 2016

ISBN: 978-0-9961605-4-4

CONTENTS

FOREWORD

"All of us are smarter than any of us." I believe this, deeply. This volume is the result of years of my own study. But it also bears the fingerprints of many of my friends.

Several of my friends are "word nerds" like me. I respect both the theological insights and communication abilities of Dan Phillips, JD Crowley, and Joe Henson. They gave of their energy and time to read through the manuscript, offering valuable suggestions that improved the book. Thank you, friends!

Thank you to Abby Huffstutler, my copy editor. You're a grammatical legalist—which is precisely what I need—but you've given me much grace.

I'm grateful to Jared and Holly Miller of Keski, LLC for their design of the cover and interior layout. Thank you for using your considerable skills to beautify the book. Thanks also to my good friend Joe Tyrpak for providing counsel and oversight of the artistic design.

You'll notice as you read through the book that I've made ample use of J. C. Ryle's commentary on John. Ryle isn't as well-known as his English contemporary, C. H. Spurgeon. But Ryle has been a dear friend to me, first through his classic book *Holiness*, then through his wonderful commentaries on the Gospels, and finally through his biography by Eric Russell.[1] I look forward to fellowshipping with him in heaven one day, and I'll thank him then for his help understanding John 4.

---

[1] Eric Russell, *J. C. Ryle: The Man of Granite with the Heart of a Child* (Ross-Shire, Scotland: Christian Focus, 2009).

Thanks to the two churches I've pastored during my John 4 studies: Tri-County Bible Church in Madison, Ohio, and Killian Hill Baptist Church in Lilburn, Georgia. You've heard bits and pieces of this book in countless sermons, and you've given me the freedom to preach John 4 at many other churches, schools, and conferences. Thank you for valuing the advance of the Kingdom beyond our immediate sphere. It has been a privilege to team with you for our Savior's glory.

Finally, thanks to my girls, to whom I dedicate this book. God has blessed me with a house *filled* with women: "Oceans of emotions." And I've loved it! Lori, thank you for partnering with me for the last twenty years. You've been a support to me, a model to our girls, and a gracious pastor's wife to those we've served together. Rebekah, Rachel, Esther, and Gracie, thank you for tolerating my borderline rude determination to get this and other projects done. The "daddy-daughter-dates" we've had when you've accompanied me on preaching trips are among the favorite times of my life. As many times as you've heard me speak of the Samaritan woman, you could probably write this book for me. You all enable me to minister more effectively than I ever could alone. You're my joy, my treasure, and my best friends. I love you!

INTRODUCTION

"I am a Samaritan woman."

If I've said that once, I've said it a thousand times. I've said it so often that it's become a joke in the two churches I've pastored. Once, while pastoring Tri-County Bible Church in Madison, Ohio, I walked out of the high school where we met, carrying a purse that someone had left behind. *"Pastor, you're taking this whole 'Samaritan woman' thing too far!"* came the heckle from my friend Fred.

I don't have gender-identity issues. But I am indeed a Samaritan woman. Here's what I mean: As I've studied John 4—a passion of mine for at least the last decade—I've identified with this ignorant, evasive, needy woman. I've come to understand that I'm as dirty and thirsty as she is. And by God's grace, I'm still as *loved* as she is—completely in spite of myself! I'm a Samaritan woman in my need, and I'd like to be a Samaritan woman in my response to the Lord Jesus.

You may assume that you know the story of the woman at the well. Perhaps you can still picture the flannelgraph images of the story from your childhood. Or you've sung songs about her, like "Fill My Cup, Lord." Perhaps the story is entirely new to you. It goes like this: Jesus meets a woman. He asks her for water. He promises her living water. She gets saved. Simple.

But it's not that simple. It's complex, and poignant, and charming, and beautiful. It's my favorite narrative from the entire Bible. Why? Because it displays the beauty of sovereign mercy. Because it's a wonderful testimony of the gospel's power. Because the story points to the answers for so many problems of our own day, such as racial prejudice, religious confusion, materialism, divorce, and sensuality.

But more than anything, John 4 is exquisite because it is a microcosm of what God is doing in the world. The purpose and process of redemption is encapsulated in this beautiful history. What God does in John 4 is illustrative of what God is doing in the world—seeking, saving, satisfying, changing, and using sinners like us. By the end of John 4, a social pariah has been transformed into a worshiper of God and one of the most effective evangelists in the entire New Testament!

Even if you've known John 4 for years, I'd like you to read it anew with me. This time, read it with fresh eyes. Notice the details. Ask yourself why it says what it says. If it's helpful, use a different Bible version than you're accustomed to in order to prevent you from moving so rapidly over the cadence of well-known phrases. Slow down. Enjoy. *Think.*

I consider the Samaritan woman a personal friend. She's often in my thoughts, and more than once she's made an appearance in my hymn texts. For that reason, at the conclusion of each chapter I've included portions of hymns I've written that fit the specific theme of that chapter. My meditations on Scripture usually come out in rhymes, and God has seen fit to use them to encourage and instruct fellow Christians. I hope they'll contribute both substance and beauty to this book.

The hymn "Come, Lonely Heart" comes directly from John 4. Greg Habegger, my fellow pastor at Killian Hill Baptist Church and my hymn-writing teammate for the last decade, has written a lovely tune for the text, which he aptly called SAMARITAN WOMAN. During a trip to Frisco, Texas, in 2012, Greg and I were blessed to hear the hymn sung at Stonebriar Community Church, where our CD *His Robes for Mine* was recorded. During the Sunday morning service, Pastor Chuck Swindoll kindly introduced us to the congregation, thanking us for writing doctrinal hymns for the church. Later in the service, he used the opening line of each stanza of the hymn in a brief gospel presentation:

Come, lonely heart.

Drink, thirsty heart.

Rest, guilty heart.

Joy, grateful heart.

There's a reason the invitations to the Samaritan woman were so easily extended to an auditorium full of people. This unnamed lady is representative of everybody. We all experience painful solitude. We all have skeletons in our closets. We all have more questions than answers. And we all have a deep thirst for something more—even if we don't know what that "something" is. By unpacking her story, we learn about ourselves. More importantly, when we study the woman at the well we engage the Man at the well—the Lord Jesus Christ—the Savior of the world.

I sincerely pray that you'll profit from this study as much as I have.

After all, I'm a Samaritan woman. And so are you!

"Come, Lonely Heart"

Come, lonely heart, to the outsider's Friend—
To Jesus, Who seeks out the lost.
Your cruel seclusion has come to an end;
Find welcome, find home, at the cross.
No soul is too small for His mercy;
No sin is too great for His grace!
Come, lonely heart, to the outsider's Friend;
Find welcome, find home, at the cross.

Drink, thirsty heart, of the water of life—
Of bountiful, soul-quenching grace.
The world's broken cisterns cannot satisfy;
The Savior is what your heart craves.
No soul is too small for His mercy;
No sin is too great for His grace!
Drink, thirsty heart, of the water of life;
The Savior is what your heart craves.

Rest, guilty heart, in forgiveness of sin—
In pardon from shame-stirring vice.
Though Satan and sinners and conscience condemn,
Your soul may be spotless as Christ.
No soul is too small for His mercy;
No sin is too great for His grace!
Rest, guilty heart, in forgiveness of sin;
Your soul may be spotless as Christ.

Joy, grateful heart, in the hope you have found—
In God, Who is seeking your praise.
Then go to the outcast, that grace may resound,
For Jesus is mighty to save.
No soul is too small for His mercy;
No sin is too great for His grace!
Joy, grateful heart, in the hope you have found,
For Jesus is mighty to save.

PART
ONE

Jesus Seeks Sinners

Now when Jesus learned that the Pharisees had heard that Jesus was making and baptizing more disciples than John (although Jesus himself did not baptize, but only his disciples), he left Judea and departed again for Galilee. And he had to pass through Samaria. So he came to a town of Samaria called Sychar, near the field that Jacob had given to his son Joseph. Jacob's well was there; so Jesus, wearied as he was from his journey, was sitting beside the well. It was about the sixth hour. A woman from Samaria came to draw water. Jesus said to her, "Give me a drink." (For his disciples had gone away into the city to buy food.) The Samaritan woman said to him, "How is it that you, a Jew, ask for a drink from me, a woman of Samaria?" (For Jews have no dealings with Samaritans.)

JOHN 4:1-9

I

A DIVINE APPOINTMENT

JOHN 4:1-6

We have perceived that he is of the substance of his mother, bone of our bone, flesh of our flesh; man in all infirmities, but not man in any guiltiness of his own; man weak, suffering, hungry, thirsty, dying, but without spot or wrinkle—pure, the immaculate Lamb of God. We have beheld him in the glory of this complex person—not God deteriorated to man, not man deified to God, but God, very God, and very man; God in all that is God-like, man in all that is manlike, and we have adored him as such.

C. H. SPURGEON[2]

The story of the Samaritan woman is an epic drama. The heroine has a history so tragic, so utterly wretched, that it reads like a novel by Charles Dickens or Victor Hugo. But the story of her miserable life is *history,* not fiction. The great Protagonist is the Lord Jesus Himself. His dialogue with the woman at the well displays the beauties and complexities of both His perfect humanity and His eternal deity. We see His weariness, His grace, His severity, and His compassion all on full display.

---

[2] Charles Haddon Spurgeon, "The Glory of Christ—Beheld!" in *Metropolitan Tabernacle Pulpit* 7 (AGES Software, 1997), 961.

The "extras" in the drama include the twelve disciples, a host of ex-husbands, and a village-full of rugged Samaritans—an entire race of outcasts.

John 4 begins, however, with a stage-setting narrative. It tells us of a hot day nearly 2000 years ago. It tells us of a solitary woman retrieving water from an ancient well. It tells us of Jesus and of His journey from Judea into Galilee.

"He Had to Pass through Samaria"

Judea describes southern Israel; Galilee describes the north. Between the two lies Samaria, the home of the despised rivals of the Jews, the Samaritans. Jesus was just passing through Samaria when He met the woman at the well. The village of Sychar was a "pit stop," not a destination for the Jews of Jesus' day—if they condescended to walk through Samaria at all. The following map will make His route clear.

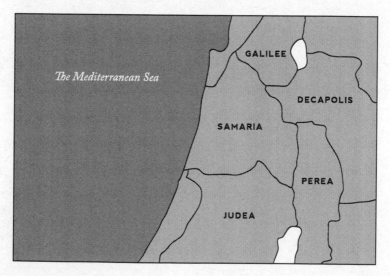

John tells us that Jesus was leaving Judea because He had been rejected by the Pharisees (vv. 1-3), the religious hypocrites who were the self-appointed conscience of the Jews. The Pharisees were interested in their traditions (as their frequent debates with Jesus about the Sabbath indicate), but they were even more interested in their power. Their defense of supposed *truth* was generally a defense of *turf*. In the first few chapters of John we learn that Jesus was no friend of the religious establishment. He introduced Himself to the religious elite in Jerusalem by making a whip and using it to scatter tables, coins, and money changers in the temple (John 2:13-22).

"Nice to make your acquaintance."

The religious leaders thought Jesus was brash. But even worse, they knew He was *popular*. John the Baptist had been frustrating enough. With his imprisonment (Mark 6:17-20), they expected a reprieve from perceived competitors. Instead, Jesus was attracting even more followers (John 3:22-26), and those disciples were identifying with Him through baptism (John 4:1-2). Where others saw a rabbi, the Pharisees saw only a rival. As He often did early in His ministry, Jesus responded to the hostility of the Jews by withdrawing. The religious muckety-mucks didn't want Him in Judea, so He departed for His native region of Galilee. En route, He would interact with—and be received by—the Samaritans. Christ's rejection by the Jews and reception by the Gentiles is another microcosm of the work of redemption, described more fully in Romans 9-11. Whereas the Jews spurned Jesus, the Gentiles embraced Him.

What a cosmic tragedy. After waiting for *millennia* for their promised Messiah, most Jews missed Him! Worse, they didn't *want* Him, if He was coming with grace rather than glory. John 1:11 can lose some of its punch due to our familiarity with it, but I wonder if John wrote it through tears: "He came to his own, and his own people did not receive him."

There are few verses so heartbreaking in the entire canon of Scripture. But verse 12 goes on to say that to all who *did* receive Him—including a lowly Samaritan woman—"he gave the right to become the children of God." John 4 is her testimony.

Color-Blind Compassion

John 4:4 says that Jesus "had to pass through Samaria." That may be a simple explanation of geography, as indicated on the map on page 20. However, Jesus could have taken a longer route and gone to Galilee by way of Perea and Decapolis to the east, avoiding Samaria altogether. Perea and Decapolis were primarily Gentile regions. Still, many self-righteous Jews did that very thing, so great was their hatred for the Samaritans.

Perhaps Jesus took the direct route through Samaria because He was in a hurry. But I think that's unlikely. After all, He ended up spending several days in Samaria (v. 40).

In light of what transpires during Jesus' journey through Samaria, I think it's safe to say that Jesus "had to pass through Samaria" because He had a divine appointment. The Greek word rendered "had to" or "must" has already been used by John in 3:7, 14, and 30. Each time, it describes a divine necessity. The necessity isn't *geographical*—it's *theological*. It's *soteriological,* focused on salvation. It's *doxological,* rooted in God's glory.

Jesus was deliberate. He was on a mission. His conversation with the woman at the well was no "chance meeting." He was prescient. He knew what was coming. He arrived at *that* well, in *that* village, at *that* time, to talk to *that* woman, by Himself—all on purpose.

So many things could have gone differently. Why not ask the disciples for a drink? Why send them all into the nearby village of Sychar, leaving Him alone? Why not go with them? The answer is clear: Jesus arranged this meeting. Why? Because Jesus seeks sinners (Luke 19:10). It's what He does. He was on a mission. Jesus knew this particular woman would be there, just as He knew her story—much to her amazement and her neighbors' (John 4:19, 29).

She isn't the only one Jesus knows so thoroughly. John 2:24-25 tells us that Jesus knows the thoughts and motives of all people. That includes this woman, His disciples, you, and me. Jesus didn't need to ask about her need, because He is God. And He wasn't turned off by her need, because He is Grace.

No soul is too small for His mercy;
No sin is too great for His grace!

Weary Omnipotence

Worn out, Jesus arrives at Jacob's well (v. 6). Yes, *that* Jacob, the father of the nation of Israel who lived around 2000 BC. Timewise, he was as far removed from Jesus as we are! Jesus arrived at Jacob's famous well around noon. That's important, as we'll see in the next chapter. But first, notice this understated phrase: "wearied as he was from his journey." Jesus was spent, so He sat down.

We should keep that in mind as we study the rest of John 4. Jesus was *tired*—but not too tired to pursue a sinner. Jesus was *tired*—but not too tired to do His Father's will and find a would-be worshiper. Jesus was *tired*—but not too tired to reprove and instruct His disciples. Jesus was *tired*—but not too tired to spend two days evangelizing an entire village.

When I read of Jesus' ministry, sometimes I feel claustrophobic. We read of His weariness in passages like Mark 6:31-35. He instructed His disciples to row Him to the other side of the Sea of Galilee, to a desolate place so they could all enjoy a respite from the work of the ministry. They needed a break. But the crowds had other plans, and they walked around and met them on the other side of the sea. What did Jesus do? He had compassion on them. Weary as He was, He spent the day ministering to them. He gave, even when it seemed He could have nothing left to give.

Another time, in Mark 5:15-34, we read of crowds pressing in on Him. Imagine that! Imagine having a mob so intent on getting your help that they push against you, reaching for you, desperate to touch you. Claustrophobic yet? I think I'd lose it: *"Get off of me! Stop touching me! Hasn't anyone taught you people about personal space?"*

But that's not Jesus. He gave, even when people were intent on taking. Touched—defiled!—by a lady with some sort of blood issue, He turned to her—not in anger, but in mercy.[3] He told her that her faith had made her well. She had audaciously

---

[3] Carl Trueman identifies the lady's illness as something related to menstruation. You can find his helpful article "Compassion for the Unclean" in *Gospel Meditations for Prayer*, ed. Chris Anderson (churchworksmedia.com, 2013), Day 3.

grasped at Him, and He responded with *grace*. That's Jesus— Grace incarnate.

We see His grace shine through His weariness again in John 4. It reminds me of the description of Gideon and his 300 men in Judges 8:4: "exhausted yet pursuing." He understands when we're bone-weary (Hebrews 4:15-16). That's encouraging. And in His fatigue He responded with mercy. That's convicting.

So Jesus was tired. It was probably a hot day for such a long journey. Weariness makes sense—except that *Jesus is God!* John's Gospel begins with a familiar phrase: "In the beginning." And it applies that quotation of Genesis 1:1 to Jesus, the eternal Word Who is God. One of John's purposes for writing his Gospel is to prove Jesus' deity (John 20:31). That's what makes John 4:6's statement that Jesus was "wearied" so stunning! Read it again, and *marvel* at it! He's the Creator. The eternal One, of Whom Isaiah says, "He does not faint or grow weary" (Isaiah 40:28). The Son Who is co-equal with the Father. And He's weary?! How can that be?

The Gospel of John abounds with proofs of Jesus' deity. He has the *attributes* of deity—from eternality to omniscience to omnipotence. He has *titles* of deity—the Son, the Lord, the Christ, the "I Am," which He repeatedly uses to describe Himself in the Gospel. He takes *prerogatives* of deity—from forgiving sins to eliciting faith to receiving worship. The book climaxes this overwhelming evidence with the conclusion that Jesus is "the Christ, the Son of God," Who alone can give eternal life (John 20:31).

But for all the proofs that Jesus is *God*, John also insists that Jesus is *man*. "The Word [Who was God; 1:1] became flesh" (1:14)! In the Lord Jesus Christ we have the perfect union of God and Man. Because He is the fusion of deity and humanity, Jesus is uniquely qualified to be the Mediator between God and man (1 Timothy 2:5). This is essential to the Christian faith, as B. B. Warfield attests:

> The doctrine of the Incarnation is the hinge on which the Christian system turns...No Incarnation, no Christianity in any distinctive sense.[4]

Jesus bridged the infinite chasm between God and man.

For the sake of illustration, try to imagine an "alternate ending" to Shakespeare's classic tragedy, *Romeo and Juliet*. Imagine if instead of committing suicide, the star-crossed lovers from rival clans had married and had a son. Imagine a baby boy named *Roliet*. No, *Juleo*. We'll go with *Julio* to give it a Spanish flair. Imagine how this baby might have united the Capulets and Montagues by merging both families into one person.

Christ did that, but to an infinitely greater degree. He is both God and man. He *reveals* the invisible God. He *redeems* the fallen man. He has combined two natures in one perfect person. "Holy God and lowly flesh in virgin's womb have joined as one!" (from my hymn "Praise Our Savior, Jesus Christ"). The paradox we find in John 4:6 where the Son of God is "wearied" is evident throughout Jesus' entire earthly life:

---

[4] Benjamin B. Warfield, *The Works of Benjamin B. Warfield*, vol. 3, *Christology and Criticism*. (Grand Rapids, MI: Baker Books, 2003), 259.

- Almighty God grew weary.
- The sovereign One sweat.
- The One Who neither slumbers nor sleeps…slept!
- The self-existent, self-sufficient One grew thirsty and hungry.
- The Creator of all things would suffer. Would bleed. Would *die!*

What a wonder the incarnation is! This normal looking Jewish man—is *God!* God—is this dusty, thirsty, sweaty *man,* seated beside the well. Both are true! That's the wonder of the incarnation. God became one of us, to rescue us. Let that inspire your worship!

"Almighty Slept"

Almighty slept. A mystery—
The Maker joined humanity.
Tucked in a stall, tossed by a storm,
Almighty slept, once weak, then worn.
Almighty slept—Who slumbers not—
And God as man salvation brought.

The Sov'reign sweat. Indignity—
The finite knew fragility.
By toil fatigued and sin oppressed,
The Sovereign sweat to bring us rest.
The Sovereign sweat great drops of red
To ponder death in sinners' stead.

Messiah wept. Such empathy—
Behold His mournful majesty.
As once He grieved by Laz'rus' tomb,
Messiah wept with death-like gloom.
Messiah wept in garden still,
Yet bowed beneath the Father's will.

The Savior bled. Oh travesty!
Yet grace has shone through agony.
While Satan scoffed and sinners scorned,
The Savior bled and died, forlorn.
The Savior bled for sin perverse
To vanquish sin and end the curse.

2

A DIVINE PURSUIT

JOHN 4:7-9

That she comes at noon, the hottest hour of the day, whispers a rumor of her reputation. The other women come at dawn, a cooler, more comfortable hour. They come not only to draw water but to take off their veils and slip out from under the thumb of a male-dominated society. They come for companionship, to talk, to laugh, and to barter gossip—much of which centers around this woman. So, shunned by Sychar's wives, she braves the sun's scorn. Anything to avoid the searing stares of the more reputable.

KEN GIRE[5]

Francis Thompson has penned a poem in which he calls God "The Hound of Heaven." The first time I heard the phrase it sounded offensive—perhaps because I'm a Westerner who hails from Colorado and not a Southerner. Someone compared God to a *hound dog?* Seriously? It sounds like a mashup of a poorly-chosen sermon illustration and an Elvis song. It sounds demeaning.

---

[5] Ken Gire, *Intimate Moments with the Savior* (Grand Rapids, MI: Zondervan, 1989), 23.

I'm not the only one whom it strikes this way. Consider this frank, yet moving description of the poem from *The Book of Verse:*

> The name is strange. It startles one at first. It is so bold, so new, so fearless. It does not attract, rather the reverse. But when one reads the poem this strangeness disappears. The meaning is understood. As the hound follows the hare, never ceasing in its running, ever drawing nearer in the chase, with unhurrying and imperturbed pace, so does God follow the fleeing soul by His Divine grace. And though in sin or in human love, away from God it seeks to hide itself, Divine grace follows after, unwearyingly follows ever after, till the soul feels its pressure forcing it to turn to Him alone in that never ending pursuit.[6]

Yes. Exactly. The description of God as the Hound of Heaven is beautiful, and it's theologically precise. Sinners don't pursue God, any more than a criminal pursues a police officer. We run *from* God, as fast and as furiously as we can. Like sheep, we are determined to go our own way (Isaiah 53:6). Not one of us seeks after God (Romans 3:11). If there's going to be a relationship between God and the sinner, it will be because God chases us down.

So what do we contribute to our salvation? The sin. The rebellion. The flight from God. H. A. Ironside writes of a young man who was questioned by a legalistic skeptic who disliked the man's testimony that God had saved him apart from any effort of his own. The older man asked the new

---

[6] *The Book of Verse* (Charlotte, NC: Neumann Press, 1988).

believer if he didn't have to do *his part* before God did His. Here's his answer:

> Oh yes, I did. For more than thirty years I ran away from God as fast as my sins could carry me. That was my part. But God took out after me and ran me down. That was His part.[7]

God pursued our rebel parents in Eden. He pursued the Samaritan woman near Sychar. And He's been pursuing sinners through the ages!

Jesus, the Great Missionary

Throughout the John 4 narrative, Jesus is the Initiator. He starts the conversation. He persists when she evades. He directs the talk to spiritual things. He keeps on His relentless pursuit even when she tries to change the subject. Jesus has set His love on this woman, in spite of her. She ducks and dodges, but He will not be denied. He is more determined to rescue her than she is to rebel. He is more determined to find her than she is to be lost. He pursues her, and eventually sovereign mercy wears her down. Jesus' rescue of the Samaritan woman is pure, undiluted grace!

If Jesus' pursuit of the Samaritan woman were an Olympic event, it wouldn't be a sprint; it would be a steeplechase! Have you seen one of those? Yes, the racers (whether humans or horses) are running. But they're also jumping over hurdles, clearing hedges, and crossing water hazards. Jesus crossed a lot

---

[7] Henry Allan Ironside, *Illustrations of Bible Truth* (n.p.: Solid Christian Books, 2014), 8. The quotation has been edited slightly for style.

of hurdles to rescue this woman, and each time He did so, He shocked people. That's what He does.

Have you ever noticed that Jesus seemed to enjoy raising eyebrows? Often in the four Gospels we read of Jesus perplexing people—whether crowds, religious leaders, or even His own disciples.

Twice in John 4 we read that Jesus surprised people by engaging the Samaritan woman. First, she herself asked (probably with some "snark" in her voice) why a Jew like Him would stoop to talk to a Samaritan like her (v. 7). Later, when the disciples returned from buying lunch in the nearby village, they were surprised that a man like Jesus would stoop to talk to a woman like her (v. 27). To their credit, the disciples didn't say what they were thinking. It must have taken everything Peter had not to speak his mind—for once!

The point is, Jesus' talk with the Samaritan woman was unexpected. There were many cultural taboos he was breaking by engaging her. By going through Samaria and by speaking to a Samaritan woman, Jesus was intentionally poking a hole in the pride and prejudice that would lead Jews to avoid Samaritans at any cost. He crossed that line on purpose. In fact, He crossed several barriers in His pursuit of the Samaritan woman.

Jesus crossed geographical barriers.

I addressed this in chapter one, but it's worth mentioning again. Consistent with the missionary spirit and border-crossing audacity Jesus would command as part of the Great Commission (Matthew 28:19-20; Mark 16:15), Jesus went into a foreign land in His pursuit of the lost.

Jesus crossed ethnic barriers.

Racial tension isn't just a modern problem. The Jews looked down upon Gentiles, but they *despised* Samaritans. Indeed, to be called a "Samaritan" was the equivalent to a four-letter-word to the Jews (John 8:48). "Jews have no dealings with Samaritans" (John 4:9) is an almost comical understatement.

The history of the Samaritans is traced back to the division of Israel into two kingdoms following the reign of King Solomon (1 Kings 12:16-24). Think of a civil war that resulted in two separate countries. Imagine the tension and hatred. But it would get worse. Whereas the Lord spared Judah (the southern kingdom) from the Assyrians, Israel succumbed to the mighty Assyrian army in 722 BC. Many of the Jews were deported. But many others were forced to intermarry with their captors (2 Kings 17:23-24). The result of this mixture of Jews and Gentiles was the Samaritan people group. The Samaritans were considered ethnic mongrels—half Jewish and half Gentile.

During the centuries between the genesis of the Samaritan people and the time of Christ, the rivalry with the Jews only worsened. The offer of the Samaritans to help rebuild the post-exilic temple was rejected by the Jews (Ezra 4:1-3). As a result, the Samaritans opposed the building of the temple (Ezra 4:4-5), much as they opposed the building of Jerusalem's walls nearly a century later (Nehemiah 2:10, 4:7, et al.).[8]

---

[8] Extrabiblical sources indicate that Sanballat, one of the villains of the book of Nehemiah, was actually the governor of Samaria. R. Dick Wilson, "Sanballat" in *The International Bible Encyclopedia*, vol. 4 (Peabody, MA: Hendrickson Publishers, 1994), 2681.

Rebuffed in their attempt to unite with the Jews to rebuild the Jerusalem temple, the Samaritans built their own temple on Mount Gerizim, possibly under the leadership of Sanballat.[9] However, that temple was destroyed in 128 BC—*by the Jews*— during the inter-testamental era. The entire history of the Jews and Samaritans was one of deeply-rooted distrust and treachery. There was a mutual avoidance and antagonism, a history of hostility that Jesus inherited—and deftly ignored. Jesus loved this woman in spite of her ethnicity.

Jesus crossed religious barriers.

The history of the Samaritan religion is inseparable from the history of the Samaritan people. When Israel split into two rival nations, King Jeroboam established a false worship system, lest the Israelites would be wooed by the king in Jerusalem when they journeyed to the temple in Jerusalem (1 Kings 12:26-33). He's not the last political ruler to use religion as a ladder to his own ambitions. Of course, Jeroboam's subjects weren't yet *ethnic* Samaritans. Still, the habit of worshiping away from Jerusalem had taken root in the region, and it would linger for centuries.

The Israelites were conquered by the Assyrians specifically because God was judging Israel for idolatry (2 Kings 17:7-23a). God's judgment didn't cure them of idolatry. Instead, the remnants who stayed in the land and married pagans attempted to worship both Jehovah and pagan idols (2 Kings 17:28-41). Eventually, around 450 BC, the Samaritans set up a rival temple at Mount Gerizim, as described above.

---

[9] W. Ewing, "Samaritans" in *The International Bible Encyclopedia*, vol. 4 (Peabody, MA: Hendrickson Publishers, 1994), 2673-74.

The Samaritan religion, like the Samaritan race, was a perverse combination of Judaism and paganism. Samaritans accepted only the Pentateuch (the first five books of the Old Testament) as the Word of God. They altered the Scriptures to direct people to Mount Gerizim instead of Mount Ebal (Jerusalem) in Deuteronomy 27:4. Jesus would say the Samaritans didn't know what they worshiped (John 4:22). A. B. Bruce calls them people "who knew not what they worshipped, and groped after God in semi-heathen darkness."[10]

Amazingly, the Samaritan religion is still being practiced today, albeit by a pathetically few faithful. I traveled to Mount Gerizim in 2010 as part of a tour of the Holy Land. My group listened to a lecture by the Samaritan high priest, complete with descriptions of blood sacrifices (which they still perform). They number only a few hundred people, and they were recently forced to bring in what I can best describe as "mail-order brides" from Europe to continue their fragile race.

Jesus rejected this false religion. But He still loved the Samaritan woman, despite her ignorance and idolatry.

Jesus crossed gender barriers.

The disciples' surprise at Jesus' public interaction with this unlikely person didn't focus on her ethnicity or religion, but on her gender. They were surprised that He spoke "with a woman" (John 4:27). Kenneth Bailey, an expert on customs in the Middle East, explains:

---

[10] A. B. Bruce, *The Training of the Twelve* (Grand Rapids, MI: Kregel, 1988), 246.

He breaks the taboo against talking to a woman, particularly in an uninhabited place with no witnesses. Throughout forty years of life in the Middle East I never crossed this social boundary line. In village society, a strange man does not even make eye contact with a woman in a public place.[11]

Jesus was expected not to look the Samaritan woman in the eyes, much less speak with her. That's hard for Westerners to imagine. However, in Jesus' day, women were valued as property rather than companions. It was a shame for a man to speak with his own wife in public! (Men, do not try this at home.) A lady would typically walk several steps behind her husband to demonstrate proper respect.

Jesus was born into a chauvinistic world. One respected teacher from the early second century BC named Ben Sirach taught men to ignore and even be wary of women, including their wives. The birth of a daughter was catastrophic to a family, offering no benefit while bringing numerous opportunities for shame.[12]

Women were downcast—but not to our Lord. Throughout His ministry, He elevated them. He spoke with them. He defended them. He commended them. He forgave them. He healed at their requests. He made them heroes of His parables. He relied on them as some of His most faithful, courageous, and generous followers.

---

[11] Kenneth E. Bailey, *Jesus Through Middle Eastern Eyes* (Downers Grove, IL: IVP Academic, 2008), 202-03.

[12] Bailey, *Jesus Through Middle Eastern Eyes,* 189-90. Bailey's description of the plight of women in Jesus' day and of Jesus' intentional elevation of women is both instructive and inspiring.

Jesus valued the Samaritan woman as a person He had made in His image. He spoke to her, He loved her, and He would use her, the unlikeliest of people, to bring revival to the Samaritans.

Jesus crossed social barriers.

If all this weren't enough, this Samaritan woman was a social pariah even among her own people. It wasn't a coincidence that she was at the well—alone—during the heat of the day. She apparently avoided people, and with good reason. John 4:18 says that she had had five husbands, and that she was now shacked up with a sixth man who hadn't bothered to marry her. Imagine having that reputation in a small town. Solitude and sunburn were nothing compared to the whispers and dirty looks that must have come from at least five groups of mothers, sisters, and "current" wives. This woman was an outcast among outcasts.

Jesus crossed moral barriers.

The Samaritan woman is about as pathetic a person as we find in the Scriptures. J. C. Ryle calls her "an ignorant, carnal-minded woman, whose moral character was more than ordinarily bad."[13] That's about right. She was notoriously sinful, and she was ashamed. She had at least six skeletons in her closet, and everybody knew about them. Her sullied reputation would have been enough to keep the rabbis of Jesus' day away from her (Luke 7:39).

---

[13] J. C. Ryle, *Expository Thoughts on the Gospels*, vol. 3 (Grand Rapids, MI: Baker Books, 2007), 201.

In spite of all that—or perhaps *because* of it—Jesus set His affection on her. He pitied her. She was sad and soiled, and He was determined that she would be saved. I love that, because *I'm a Samaritan woman.* If Jesus could love her—could *forgive* her—there's hope for people like me and you, regardless of what we've done, from extortion to abortion.

No soul is too small for His mercy;
No sin is too great for His grace!

Jesus loves broken people. He came to seek and to save the lost (Luke 19:10). He came into the world to save filthy sinners like us (1 Timothy 1:15), and by saving the very worst of us He shows His ability to save *any* of us (1 Timothy 1:16). That's the lesson we learn from the woman at the well, the object of Christ's affection and a trophy of His power to save. Ryle's insights are again worth repeating:

> We must never despise any soul after reading this passage. None can be worse than this woman. But Christ did not despise her. We must never despair of any soul after reading this passage. If this woman was converted, anyone may be converted.[14]

Jesus is Omnigracious

All of this barrier-crossing and sacred-cow-kicking was entirely normal for Jesus. Sometimes we imagine Jesus with a frowning face and a furrowed brow. We imagine Him being austere, or intimidating, or holier-than-thou.

---

[14] Ryle, *Expository Thoughts*, 227.

He is holier than us, of course. But He is also *omnigracious.* If that's not a word, it should be. Jesus has an infinite supply of grace, and He heaps it upon undeserving, *ill-*deserving sinners like us: "grace upon grace" (John 1:16). He saved His harsh words for religious hypocrites, but He welcomed even notorious sinners. Though He occasionally taught multitudes, He did His best work in private, one person at a time.

And more times than not, He engaged *outcasts.* He touched a leper (Matthew 8:1-4). He healed blind men the crowds had tried to hush (Matthew 20:29-34). He tamed a crazy, naked demoniac (Mark 8:35). He healed the servant of a Roman centurion (Matthew 8:5-13) and the daughter of a humble Syrophoenician woman (Mark 7:24-30). Perhaps stooping further than ever, He even healed Peter's mother-in-law (Matthew 8:14-15).[15]

Time fails me to provide an exhaustive list of the outsiders, rejects, and sinners Jesus welcomed, and even sought. He forgave prostitutes. He welcomed children whom even His own disciples had dismissed as a nuisance. He went to the homes of publicans, the hated and traitorous tax collectors of His day. What the Pharisees and scribes said as a condemnation is gloriously true: "This man receives sinners" (Luke 15:2). Jesus is "the friend of tax collectors and sinners" (Luke 7:34). And praise God that He is!

Different...but the Same

I'll close this chapter with what I believe is an intentional and stunning contrast. The record of Jesus' interaction with the

---

[15] Just kidding, mothers-in-law!

Samaritan woman in John 4 follows immediately on the heels of Jesus' interview with Nicodemus in John 3. It's an amazing juxtaposition. The two couldn't be more different. They represent the poles of society:

- He's a Jew. She's a Samaritan.
- He's a man. She's a woman.
- He's respected as "*the* teacher in Israel" (3:10). She's reviled as an outcast even in Samaria.
- He's impeccably educated. She's ignorant.
- He's wealthy. She's impoverished.
- He's famous. She's infamous.
- He's outwardly righteous. She's outright rebellious.

Still, the Lord Jesus treats them exactly the same. He looks past gender, race, religion, and social standing, and He sees two sinners. The rabbi was as lost as the rebel. The serious Pharisee was no better than the serial divorcee. That's what Jesus means when He tells Nicodemus, "You must be born again" (John 3:3, 7). That sounds lofty, but what it really means is this: *"You're a spiritual corpse, Rabbi. You're dead, and you need new life."*

This is a profound lesson. It speaks to all of us, whether we relate more to self-righteous Nicodemus or the unrighteous woman at the well. The lesson is this: *No one is too holy to need God's grace or too lowly to receive it.*

If ever anyone were beyond the *need* of grace, Nicodemus would be the person. And if ever anyone were beyond the *reach* of grace, the Samaritan woman would be that person. Yet, Jesus told both the lofty Jew and the lowly Samaritan of their spiritual needs. And Jesus graciously met those needs. The gospel levels the playing field. It removes barriers.

As my friend J. D. Crowley has beautifully said, "The Gospel of Jesus Christ will plunge a cross-shaped dagger right into the heart of racism."[16] Indeed it does, and it should kill prejudice in our hearts, as well. From every tribe, tongue, kindred, and nation, Jesus is weaving a beautiful, multi-colored tapestry of grace!

Let this lesson alter your self-identity. I often remind the people I pastor at Killian Hill Baptist Church that "we're not the good people." We're sinners. We're no better than anyone else. But for God's grace, we'd be hell-bent and hell-bound.

Paul—the greatest missionary the world has ever known!—identified himself as "the chief of sinners" (1 Timothy 1:15b). And he did so just a few verses after providing a depravity list of grievous sins (1 Timothy 1:8-11). He had just spoken of thieves, fornicators, homosexuals, and slave traders, and he still concluded that he was the worst sinner he knew. I'm almost tempted to put a new slogan on our church website: *"Killian Hill Baptist Church: We're a Mess!"* Thankfully, "Christ Jesus came into the world to save sinners"—including Samaritan women like us (1 Timothy 1:15a)!

> *No soul is too small for His mercy;*
> *No sin is too great for His grace!*

Christian, never forget that you don't approach God on the basis of your performance. You're not allowed to pray

---

[16] J. D. Crowley, "Check It Off the List" in *Gospel Meditations for Missions*, ed. Chris Anderson (churchworksmedia.com, 2011), Day 6.

because you've been good, and you're not prohibited from praying because you've been bad. The truth is, you've *never* really had a "good day" spiritually, at least not by God's standards. You approach God as a guilty sinner—every day—and you do so on the basis of His Son. You approach God in Jesus' name (John 14:13-14), claiming His merit and not your own.

If you're not yet a Christian, I'm so thankful that you've read this far. My prayer is that you'll come to understand that God loves you so much He sacrificed His own perfect Son to rescue you from sin and to gain you for Himself. It's an amazing love story, and best of all, it's absolutely true. Keep reading!

"Relentless Love"

Relentless love pursued my heart,
though I would hide—
Was unreturned, yet undeterred by pride.
Till by a grace unsought, my rebel soul was caught—
Redeemed by love that would not be denied.

Unbounded love, unfailing love,
Love raised upon a tree;
Unending love, prevailing love—
My Savior's sovereign love for me.

"Every Knee Shall Bow"

Every tribe shall come to Thee,
Worthy Lamb, so speak through me.
Kingdoms, kindreds, tribes, and tongues—
Out of each shall praise be sung.
Make from every shade and race
A tapestry of lavish grace!
Every tribe shall come to Thee,
Worthy Lamb, so speak through me.

PART

TWO

Jesus Saves Sinners

———————————————————————

Jesus answered her, "If you knew the gift of God, and who it is that is saying to you, 'Give me a drink,' you would have asked him, and he would have given you living water."

JOHN 4:10

The woman said to him, "I know that Messiah is coming (he who is called Christ). When he comes, he will tell us all things." Jesus said to her, "I who speak to you am he."

JOHN 4:25-26

3

THE BAD SAMARITAN

JOHN 4:10-26

Till men and women are brought to feel their sinfulness and need, no real good is ever done to their souls. Till a sinner sees himself as God sees him, he will continue careless, trifling, and unmoved. By all means we must labour to convince the unconverted man of sin, to prick his conscience, to open his eyes, to show him himself. To this end we must expound the length and breadth of God's holy law. To this end we must denounce every practice contrary to that law, however fashionable and customary. This is the only way to do good. Never does a soul value the Gospel medicine until it feels its disease. Never does a man see any beauty in Christ as a Saviour, until he discovers that he is himself a lost and ruined sinner.

J. C. RYLE[17]

Jesus was the master Evangelist. He didn't have a canned approach or a memorized script. The gospel flowed from His mouth with complete naturalness. Indeed, it *overflowed*—He couldn't contain it.

---

[17] Ryle, *Expository Thoughts*, 204.

Sometimes, as with Nicodemus, He cut the small talk and went straight to the chase. Nicodemus, so timid that he came to Jesus by night lest his fellow Pharisees should criticize Him, tiptoed around Jesus, offering Him a compliment as an ice-breaker (John 3:1-2). Jesus didn't return the favor, but instead made a no-nonsense proclamation:

> Jesus answered him, "Truly, truly, I say to you, unless one is born again he cannot see the kingdom of God" (John 3:3).

Nicodemus initially failed to understand or believe. He seemed, in fact, to turn Jesus' sober word into a joke. So Jesus rebuked him even more directly: "Are you the teacher of Israel and yet you do not understand these things?" (John 3:10).

That's not exactly a page from *How to Win Friends and Influence People.* Jesus didn't welcome the esteemed rabbi's support. He didn't flatter him. Jesus blew him up: *"Nicodemus, you're dead. And you're dumb."*

Thankfully, the wind of the Spirit was blowing on the heart of Nicodemus (John 3:8), and he eventually believed. He was indeed born again by trusting in Jesus—not morality or religion—as his only hope of salvation. He evidenced his new spiritual life with new spiritual courage. When his fellow Pharisees crucified Jesus, Nicodemus helped Joseph of Arimathea care for Jesus' dead body—an act of devotion to his Savior and defiance to his peers (John 19:39). Jesus knew just the approach that Nicodemus needed, for He knows the hearts of all men (John 2:24-25; Acts 15:8).

Jesus approaches the woman at the well with more caution. This time, He starts the conversation, and He does so with surprising kindness. His asking her for a drink isn't just requesting a favor for Himself; it's treating her with respect and expressing acceptance to her. As He has nothing with which to gain a drink Himself (John 4:11), He is essentially asking to share her cup—a gesture as full of grace as His touching a leper.

Jews didn't talk to Samaritans (John 4:9). They certainly didn't drink after them. Imagine the segregated drinking fountains of the pre-civil-rights South in the United States. Think of Rosa Parks' shunning of societal norms on that bus in Montgomery, Alabama, on December 1, 1955. Gestures like this are powerful. By asking for a drink, Jesus is willing to be put socially in her debt. He is indicating to the woman that He comes as a friend, not an oppressor.

Literally Figurative

Immediately after asking her for a drink, Jesus brilliantly turns the conversation in the direction of the gospel. He tells her that if she knew Who He really was, *she* would be the one making a request, and it would be for "living water" (John 4:10). He moves from a physical illustration to a spiritual lesson. And she doesn't get it. People seldom did the first time. Consider how many times Jesus' object lessons were missed in John's Gospel:

- Jesus promised to rebuild the temple in three days after the Jews destroyed it; they understood Him to be speaking of the physical temple and missed the allusion to His body (John 2:19-22).

- Jesus told Nicodemus he needed to be born again; Nicodemus asked the comical question if he must in fact reenter his mother's womb, missing Jesus' point that while he had physical life, he lacked spiritual life (John 3:1-9).

- Jesus told His disciples He had "food to eat" that they knew nothing of; they assumed someone had ordered Him carry-out, missing His point, that He was preoccupied with doing His Father's will (John 4:31-34).

- Jesus told the multitudes they would need to eat His flesh and drink His blood; they took Him literally (eww!) and missed His call to saving faith, choosing instead to leave Him (John 6:51-60, 66).

Jesus used analogies that were close at hand. In doing so, He modeled what redemptive conversations look like. His evangelistic strategy was simple. My friend David Hosaflook puts it this way: *"Pray. Meet people. Tell them about Jesus."* Learn from your Savior. Talk to people. Look them in the eye. Surprise them with your interest. Disarm them with your kindness. Ask for or offer a favor. Question them. Listen to them. As another missionary friend has said, *"Learn the story behind the face."* And when the opportunity is right, turn the conversation to Christ.

If You Knew...

In John 4, Jesus' illustration is water. He says that whereas He asks the woman to meet His physical need, He is able to meet her spiritual, eternal need. Christ's words from John 4:10 are haunting to me:

If you knew the gift of God, and who it is that is saying to you, "Give me a drink," you would have asked him, and he would have given you living water.

"If you knew." There's the rub. *If. You. Knew.* We are surrounded by people who are lost in sin. Religious or reckless, they are damned without Christ. They have no hope of forgiveness, of reconciliation, of heaven. But they would, "if they knew."

This is what brings urgency to the gospel message. They need to know Who Jesus is! They need to know their own need. They need to know to ask Him to meet that need. And according to Jesus, if they hear, if they *know,* many will repent and believe. The fact that billions of people *don't* know is what makes evangelism and missions so urgent. It is indeed great news that "everyone who calls on the name of the Lord will be saved" (Romans 10:13). But that good news gives way to a heartbreaking, soul-stirring series of questions:

> How then will they call on him in whom they have not believed? And how are they to believe in him of whom they have never heard? And how are they to hear without someone preaching? And how are they to preach unless they are sent? As it is written, "How beautiful are the feet of those who preach the good news!" But they have not all obeyed the gospel. For Isaiah says, "Lord, who has believed what he has heard from us?" So faith comes from hearing, and hearing through the word of Christ (Romans 10:14-17).

Faith comes by hearing the word of Christ. There will be no faith apart from people hearing the gospel. And there will be no hearing apart from Christians who follow the example of Jesus and "preach the good news" to those who most need to hear it. Don't let the word "preach" confuse you. No ordination is necessary. We're not talking about standing behind a wooden pulpit on a Sunday morning. Just understand the gospel, and tell people about it. Open your mouth and talk. *"Pray. Meet people. Tell them about Jesus."*

If they could hear—if they *knew*—they would ask Him for the infinitely gracious gift of salvation! And *you* could be the means of their knowing! In light of the ignorance that condemns the lost, J. C. Ryle calls the church to evangelistic action:

> Let it be a settled principle in our minds that the first and chief business of the Church of Christ is to preach the Gospel.[18]

Thankfully, by the time Jesus' conversation with the Samaritan woman concludes, she does know. Whereas Jesus sometimes spoke to Jews with veiled and cryptic language, He reveals Himself to the woman at the well with startling candor. He "connects the dots for her." And it's fascinating to watch it unfold.

I Am

Early in their meeting, she knows Jesus is unique. He *actually spoke* to her. He's not a typical Jew, that's for sure. Beyond that, He's not a typical man—and if there is one thing she knows, it's men! No, Jesus is special.

His offer of "living water" piques her interest, especially because He has nothing with which to draw (John 4:11a). Interested, she asks for more information: "Where do you get

---

[18] Ryle, *Expository Thoughts*, 204.

this living water?" (John 4:11b). Without awaiting an answer she poses another, bolder question: "Are you greater than our father Jacob?" (John 4:12). Jacob had dug this well some 2000 years ago. The well had sustained people and livestock for two millennia. Was Jesus claiming to provide something even greater?

I love this! It's an insightful question. She's not yet saved. She lacks understanding. But the wind of the Spirit is blowing, as it had with Nicodemus (John 3:8).

Notice Jesus' answer. First, He doesn't mock the Samaritans' claiming of Jacob as their father, as most Jews would have done. Second, He answers in the affirmative: "Yes, I'm greater than Jacob!" He doesn't come right out and say it yet, but He says that all who drink from Jacob's well will thirst again (v. 13). However, whoever drinks from Jesus' well—from the gospel of saving grace—will never thirst again (v. 14).

Don't miss a single word of Jesus' claim and invitation. He moves the conversation from the temporary to the eternal. He moves the conversation from the patriarchs to the Promised One. He speaks not of earning salvation but of receiving it as a gift: "Whoever drinks of the water *that I will give him* will never be thirsty again" (v. 14). Salvation cannot be earned. No rope is long enough to reach the depths of the waters of true salvation. No effort can pull that water up. It can only be received as a gift from the Lord Jesus. Ah, but it is available for the asking—to "whomever." Even an ignorant, ashamed, sinful Samaritan woman!

She's interested. She wants what He offers. But she still can't shake the physical in favor of the spiritual. She asks for the water He offers (John 4:15a). *Great!* And she wants it so she will no longer have to come to the well to draw water (John 4:15b). *Ugh!*

She doesn't get it—not yet. Nevertheless, Jesus answers her request and advances the conversation. He speaks of her shameful past (which we'll cover in the next several chapters). This piques her interest yet again—and also makes her profoundly uncomfortable. He knows her. He can read her mind and rehearse her past! His omniscience will be the very thing she highlights to her neighbors later in the chapter: "Come see a man that told me all that I ever did!" (John 4:29, 39).

Imagine her mental recap: *"He's not just kind—for a Jew. He's more than a great man—even greater than Jacob. So what is He?"* She gives her best guess in verse 19: "Sir, I perceive that you are a prophet." That's not a small step for her, because the Samaritans didn't recognize the Old Testament prophets as legitimate. Whether or not she knows the depth of her statement, she's wondering if Jesus is the "prophet like Moses" promised in Deuteronomy 18:15 and 18—Scriptures the Samaritans did value. She's getting warmer.

Their conversation moves to her marital history. It moves again—abruptly, since she's dodging—to the proper venue for worship. But let's keep tracking her *understanding of Jesus*. She's called Jesus a prophet (v. 19). Now, as her conversation with Him concludes, she speaks of the Promised Savior: "I know that Messiah is coming.... When He comes, He will tell us all things" (John 4:25). This is a hard verse to understand. She may be shrugging off the conversation, essentially saying, "We won't know the answers to these questions until the Messiah comes." But in light of Jesus' candid response, I think she's saying more—the very question she would pose to her fellow Samaritans only a few minutes later: "Can this be the Christ?" (John 4:29).

Again, imagine her thought process as the conversation continues: *"He's kind. He's great. He's knowledgeable. He's a prophet—at the very least. But is He more? Dare I ask? Is He the promised and awaited Messiah? I'll state it in a non-committal way and see how He responds."* She clears her throat, and with a watchful eye she says, "When the Messiah comes, He will tell us."

Jesus meets her gaze. He sees her hope. And for the first time in John's Gospel and with clarity unprecedented in the other Gospels, He affirms His identity to her: "I who speak to you am he" (John 4:26).

She was right! Jesus *is* the Messiah! He said so in unmistakable terms. In fact, He not only claimed to be the Messiah. His specific answer, literally translated from the Greek text, was "I Am." The pronoun "he" was added by English translators in an attempt to clarify the statement. I'm not sure they succeeded. What Jesus actually says is "I Am," duplicating the self-revelation of God to Moses at the burning bush (Exodus 3:14). Jesus is claiming to be none other than Jehovah! The Gospel of John contains many such "I Am" statements—and this is the *first*.

To whom does Jesus make this unprecedented disclosure? To Rabbi Nicodemus? No. To the delinquent disciples? Not yet. No, He gives this soul-saving information to the humblest and least "qualified" of hearers—the Samaritan woman. John MacArthur reflects on this gracious self-revelation:

Jesus' revelation of Himself to this woman demonstrated that God's saving love knows no limitations; it transcends all barriers of race, gender, ethnicity, and religious tradition. In contrast to human love, divine love is indiscriminate and all-encompassing (cf. 3:16). That Jesus chose to make Himself known first not only to a Samaritan, but also to a woman, was a stinging rebuke to members of Israel's religious elite—who rejected Him even when He did reveal Himself to them.[19]

Remember the haunting but hope-filled words of John 4:10:

If you knew the gift of God, and who it is that is saying to you, "Give me a drink," you would have asked him, and he would have given you living water.

If she knew, she would ask. Now she does know, and I believe this is the very moment when she asked for and received the gift of salvation!

---

[19] John MacArthur, *The MacArthur New Testament Commentary: John 1-11* (Chicago: Moody, 2006), 140.

"Your Beauty Fills Our Eyes"

We have looked in faith to Christ,
Beholding God's atoning Lamb.
He for our sins was sacrificed,
Thus we, though dead, have been born again.

Jesus, Your beauty fills our eyes—
First looking, we were justified;
Now gazing deeper sanctifies,
Till face to face, we are glorified.

4

NO CONDEMNATION

JOHN 4:16-18

*[A] gospel without propitiation at its heart is another
gospel than that which Paul preached.*

*The wrath of God is as personal, and as potent, as his Love;
and, just as the blood-shedding of the Lord Jesus was the
direct manifesting of his Father's love toward us, so it was
the direct averting of his Father's wrath against us.*

*Jesus Christ has shielded us from the nightmare prospect of
retributive justice by becoming our representative substitute, in obedience to his Father's will, and receiving
the wages of our sin in our place.*

J. I. PACKER[20]

I have four children. Specifically, I have four *girls*. Very soon
I will have four *teenaged* girls. I often complain about how
tough it is to be so outnumbered. But the truth is, I have an
amazing relationship with each of them. It's good to be me. I

---

[20] J. I. Packer, *Knowing God* (Downers Grove, IL: InterVarsity Press, 1993), 182, 184, 189.
Packer's chapter on the doctrine of propitiation, called "The Heart of the Gospel," is a classic presentation of the doctrine. I highly commend it.

wouldn't change a thing. There's a special bond between a dad and his daughter, or at least there ought to be.

My family is fluent in playful sarcasm. We don't bludgeon each other with sarcasm, or even slice and dice. We just enjoy some healthy banter. We're not great athletes, but if sass were an Olympic sport, we could probably medal. (Would-be suitors, you've been warned!)

Occasionally my girls will respond to my insightful commentary on life with this dreaded judgment: *"Wow, Dad. That was random."* They assume—probably because they can't yet keep up with their dad's superior wit—that I've said something off-topic. *"Where'd that come from?!"*

Well, I imagine that Jesus' request that the Samaritan woman retrieve her husband strikes her as completely random. She asks for the very thing He offers—water which satisfies eternally—and He responds by telling her to go get her husband (vv. 15-16). *Where'd that come from?!*

In reality, Jesus wasn't changing the subject. His very pointed question is the beginning of His answer to her request for living water. He would indeed meet her need. But first He had to *reveal* it—to her!

Severe Mercy: Jesus Exposes Her Sin Without Condemning Her

In chapter 2, I described Jesus as *omnigracious*. He isn't turned off by severely needy people, regardless of whether they have a contagious disease or a toxic reputation. Jesus "receives sinners" (Luke 15:2). He came to seek and save sinners (1 Timothy 1:15), not condemn them (John 3:17).[21]

Although the Lord deals mercifully with sinners, His is a *severe* mercy. He graciously drags her sin into the open so that He can address it.

Prompted by a loving desire to free her from her bondage to sin, Jesus gives her an opportunity to confess. He doesn't accuse her; He commands her: "Go, call your husband, and come here" (v. 16).

She's been given the opportunity to come clean, but instead she evades: "I have no husband" (v. 17). Suddenly, she's not so chatty. Her answer is curt—just three words in Greek. *Technically*, she's correct. She's a five-time divorcee who is now shacked up with a man not her husband. She's...umm...*single*.

Having given her the chance to acknowledge her condition herself, Jesus now takes the direct route and reveals what He miraculously knows:

> You are right in saying, "I have no husband"; for you have had five husbands, and the one you now have is not your husband. What you have said is true (vv. 17-18).

Ouch. Imagine hearing a description of your darkest secrets, with pinpoint accuracy, from the lips of a stranger. I'm sure her heart immediately filled with shame and fear. I wonder if there was also a bit of hope. Jesus' omniscience certainly made an impression on her; she couldn't stop telling others

---

[21] If we're not careful, we'll interpret texts that highlight Jesus' compassion on sinners in a way that minimizes sin. Those who embrace grace will always run that risk. Full-orbed grace—understanding that my obedience *doesn't ever earn God's favor*—can result in the devastating error of antinomianism—the belief that my obedience as a saved man *doesn't matter*. But that's not the case! Obedience doesn't earn God's favor, but it does evidence that His grace is active in our lives. Obedience doesn't cause conversion, but it certainly follows it. Grace teaches *godliness* (Titus 2:11)!

about it once her talk with Jesus ended (John 4:29, 39). Jesus was amazing...and she was *busted.*

The twenty-first century church could learn a great deal from Jesus' treatment of this woman's sin. He loved her, but it wasn't the toothless sentimentality which masquerades as love in our day. Jesus didn't love her so much that He *ignored* her sin. Indeed, He loved her so much that He *didn't* ignore it; He *exposed* it to her—and loved her regardless! He allowed her to see her sin to be inexcusably vile. He didn't bring the balm of His grace until He brought the lance of the Law. She was immoral. Guilty. Condemned. Without excuse. And she needed to own it before she could be saved from it.

Grace never sidesteps sin. Nor do grace-giving preachers. The gospel preaching in the book of Acts didn't warm people with messages about God's loving plan for their lives. No, it crushed them.

The way Peter incessantly reminds the Jews of their guilt in Acts 2 through 5 is almost comical. It's like he can't even mention the name Jesus without adding a stinging indictment: *"whom you crucified!"* (Acts 2:23, 36; 3:13-15; 4:10; 5:30). He allowed people to stew in the juices of their own depravity. He intentionally kept back the remedy until they were convicted of their sin and saw their hopeless condition. He withheld a word of grace until their consciences were battered.

For example, in Acts 2:37a, the ESV says Peter's hearers were "cut to the heart"—a much bloodier rendering than the KJV's "pricked." Guilt-ridden and desperate, they pleaded with the apostles for a solution: "Brothers, what shall we do?" (Acts 2:37b). Then—only after Scripture-informed, Spirit-induced conviction of sin—Peter pointed them to the saving grace of Jesus and urged them to believing repentance and its accompanying sign of baptism (Acts 2:38).

Jonathan Edwards' famous message *Sinners in the Hands of an Angry God* sounds strange to our modern ears. Imagine hearing Joel Osteen tell people that their souls hang over hell much like a spider being suspended over a candle! Can you? Edwards probably didn't flash a toothy smile while delivering that message.

The preachers of the First Great Awakening in the United States (c. 1730 – c. 1743) made a habit of preaching the Law before preaching the gospel. As odd as it sounds to us, they would "preach terrors," confronting sinners with their condemnation and God's coming wrath. They would offer the healing words of forgiveness through Christ only to those who evidenced deep conviction of sin and returned for spiritual help after the meeting had concluded. They knew the God-ordained power and purpose of the Law to drive conscience-stricken sinners to Christ (Galatians 3:27), and they used it well.[22]

Jesus—with severe mercy—highlights the Samaritan's sin, but He stops short of condemning her. It is as if He lays down the X-ray showing the deadly tumor, and then simply awaits her response.

It's very like His encounter with the woman caught in the act of adultery in John 8:1-8. Jesus—the only one with the

---

[22] For a compelling description of the preaching which God used in the First Great Awakening, I highly commend Iain H. Murray's great book, *Revival and Revivalism* (Carlisle, PA: Banner of Truth, 1994).

moral standing to accuse and condemn either woman—essentially says to both, "Neither do I condemn you."

No soul is too small for His mercy;
No sin is too great for His grace!

Jesus didn't condemn sinners. That's beautiful. And potentially blasphemous.

Really? Really.

Jesus didn't have the prerogative of simply *excusing* sin. As my friend Dan Phillips often says, "The gospel is not God's way of saying that sin is OK." Jesus' mission wasn't to "lower the bar." He specifically condemned "whoever relaxes one of the least of these commandments and teaches others to do the same" (Matthew 5:19). His grace isn't a shrug or a wink that simply lets the guilty go free. That's not grace at all. It's evil. It's blasphemy.

Imagine your outrage if the man who murdered your child was simply pardoned of his crime by a judge who felt like extending "grace." A judge has no right to pervert justice in the name of mercy. No one does, including God Himself. Proverbs 17:15 says that the one who "justifies the wicked... [is] an abomination to the Lord." That's a startling statement in light of New Testament teaching that *God justifies the ungodly* (Romans 4:5). How can God maintain His justice while pardoning sinners? How could Jesus expose the Samaritan woman's sin, yet not condemn her? How can He do the same for you? The answer is wonderful—and devastating.

Sacrificial Mercy: Jesus Forgave Her Sin by Being Condemned for Her

Jesus didn't simply erase the woman's substantial sin record by an executive order. That would be a perversion of justice. It would rock the very foundations of the throne of God (Psalm 89:14).

Instead, Jesus *paid for her sins,* in full. He could only pardon the Samaritan woman because He would be "pierced for [her] transgressions" (Isaiah 53:5a). He could only say "neither do I condemn you" to the adulterous woman because He would be "crushed for [her] iniquities" (Isaiah 53:5b). He can heap no condemnation on those who are in Christ Jesus because "upon Him was the chastisement that brought us peace" (Romans 8:1; Isaiah 53:5c). He can forgive you and me because "with His wounds we are healed" (Isaiah 53:5d). That is the genius of the gospel—the very thing that allows God to maintain His justice even as He justifies the wicked (Romans 3:26).

Jesus came not to condemn us (John 3:17), but to save us by *being* condemned Himself (John 3:16).

The salvation of Samaritan women like us rests on both the *life* and *death* of Christ. Both are essential to the "Great Exchange" of our salvation. This is crucial truth, so let's take a little time to unpack it.

We are saved by Jesus' vicarious life—justification.

Although we sing almost exclusively about Jesus' death, Scripture teaches that His *life* was equally essential to our redemption. Acts 10:38 gives us a memorable summary of Jesus' earthly ministry: "He went about doing good." Some have assumed that

that's *all* Jesus did. He provided us an example of selfless living: "WWJD: What would Jesus do?"

But His life was more than a model. He didn't just perform "random acts of kindness." He perfected righteousness.

One example of this comes from the record of Jesus' baptism. John the Baptist understandably felt unworthy to baptize Jesus. But in His explanation of His need to identify with humanity even by being baptized, Jesus said, "Let it be so for now, for thus it is fitting for us to fulfill all righteousness" (Matthew 3:15). Jesus' baptism—like the rest of His earthly life—"fulfilled righteousness" in our stead. He obeyed God's commands on our behalf.

The Father and Spirit demonstrated their approval of Jesus in a Trinitarian display: as the Son emerged from the water, the Spirit descended on Him in a form like a dove, and the Father spoke audibly from heaven (Matthew 3:15-17). All three persons of the Trinity acted— distinctly from each other—at the same time! So much for the heresy of Modalism, which teaches that God is but one person Who appears in various forms at various times.

Beyond proving the Trinity, however, the content of the Father's words are vital: "This is my beloved Son, *with whom I am well pleased"* (Matthew 3:17). The Father was pleased with the Son—not only in His perfections as the Son of God, but in His perfect obedience as the Son of *Man*. In His human life, Jesus always pleased the Father (John 8:39).

Matthew 5:17-20 advances this idea. During His famous Sermon on the Mount, Jesus made it clear that He didn't come to abolish the Law (v. 17) or even to relax it (v. 19). Instead,

He came to "fulfill" both the requirements of the Law and the predictions of the Prophets (vv. 17-18). Lest we miss the significance of Jesus fulfilling the Law on our behalf—vicariously obeying the commands we do not—Jesus told us that superhuman obedience is required if we would enter His Kingdom:

> For I tell you, unless your righteousness exceeds that of the scribes and Pharisees, you will never enter the kingdom of heaven (v. 20).

That's not possible. Not for sinners like you and me! Not for Samaritan women! Yet Jesus required God-like perfection (Matthew 5:48). Only Jesus could achieve perfect obedience—and He did. He lived in our place, as our substitute. He kept every single Law of God, and He offers His perfect righteousness to us if we will but believe in Him as our Savior.

Paul addressed this need for what is sometimes called an "alien" righteousness—that is, righteousness from outside of ourselves—in Romans 10:1-4. Paul was burdened for the Jews, who were religiously zealous but ignorant (vv. 1-2). That's ironic, in light of the fact that Jesus described the religious Samaritans the same way in John 4:22. Paul lamented the Jews' pride, which led them to empty efforts to establish their own righteousness rather than admitting their need of *God's* righteousness—a righteousness which would be credited to them only if they had faith in Christ (v. 3; see Romans 3:22).

Paul then moved immediately to the role of Christ in providing that righteousness—the *human* righteousness that comes from perfect obedience to God's Law: "For Christ is the end of the law for righteousness to everyone who believes" (Romans 10:4).

Christ is the *goal* and *culmination* of the Law. He kept the Law, flawlessly. And the righteousness He earned by His obedience is imputed (or credited) to Christians who repent of both their personal *righteousness* and *unrighteousness* and cling to Jesus alone as their hope of salvation.

My friend and mentor Michael Barrett helped me to understand the importance of Jesus' vicarious (substitutionary) life—what theologians call His "active obedience"—in his wonderful book, *Complete in Him*. Speaking of the righteousness imputed to the repentant believer, Barrett writes the following:

> I must clarify that I am not referring to the inherent and eternal righteousness that Christ has by virtue of His deity. It is wonderfully true that as God He is righteous. But the righteousness that "counts" for our salvation is that which He earned every day and every moment for the thirty-some years He lived on earth.[23]

What sinners need is what Paul describes in Philippians 3. Though eminently religious (Philippians 3:4-11), Paul repented of His own vain religious performance and depended entirely on Christ:

> …not having a righteousness of my own that comes from the law, but that which comes through faith in Christ, the righteousness from God that depends on faith (Philippians 3:9).

---

[23] Michael P. V. Barrett, *Complete in Him* (Greenville, SC: Ambassador-Emerald International, 2000), 132.

Christ's perfect life provides the righteousness we lack. Christians are clothed in His righteousness as in a robe (Isaiah 61:10; 2 Corinthians 5:21). God looks on us and sees Christ. It is no blasphemy, then, to say that when God looks on me, He says, "This is my beloved son, in whom I am well pleased." In spite of me. Because of Christ!

I recently wrote of this glorious truth in "The Father Looks on Me," a hymn for which my daughter Rebekah composed an exquisite tune:

> *The Father looks on me and sees*
> *Not what I was or am;*
> *He views the righteousness of Christ,*
> *And not my cursèd sin.*

> *The Father looks and pities me;*
> *He knows that I am dust.*
> *He treats me not as I deserve,*
> *But as though I were just.*

> *The Father looks on me and smiles,*
> *For it is Christ He sees;*
> *"This is my own belovèd son,*
> *In Whom I am well pleased."*

That's half the equation. Jesus provides the righteousness we lack. But what about the unrighteousness we possess? What about our sin? What about the Samaritan woman's sin?

We are saved by Jesus' vicarious death—propitiation.

When Jesus died, He wasn't just slain by a Jewish mob, or religious conspirators, or Roman guards. Scripture makes it clear that Jesus was crushed by God the Father (Isaiah 53:10). On the cross, God the Father was *estranged* from God the Son. And God the Father *executed* God the Son. The sins of the Samaritan woman—and of Samaritan women like us—required punishment. *Sinners* have earned God's wrath, and *God Himself* absorbed it. That's stunning.

Jesus placed Himself in the middle of a cosmic crossfire. From the human side, Jesus absorbed sin. He was "made to be sin for us" though He Himself "knew no sin" (2 Corinthians 5:21). The sinless One was shrouded in sin. The One Who can't even *look* on sin (Habakkuk 2:13), in Whom there is no darkness at all (1 John 1:5), was *immersed* in our sin on the cross.

We can't fathom how devastating that must have been for the One Whom angels praise as "Holy! Holy! Holy!" Think of your own sin—how shameful and disgusting it is, even to you who are all-too-accustomed to it. Multiply it by millions. By billions. Imagine the trauma of the sinless Son of God being sullied by it. R. C. Sproul speaks the unspeakable:

> At the moment when Christ took on Himself the sin of the world, His figure on the cross was the most grotesque, most obscene mass of concentrated sin in the history of the world.[24]

Again, Jesus inserted Himself into the absolute center of an infinite crossfire. From humanity, Jesus absorbed sin. And from God the Father, Jesus absorbed wrath.

That's a vital statement: Jesus *absorbed* God's wrath. He didn't erase it. He didn't lessen it. He didn't even deflect it. He *absorbed* it. That's the meaning of the word "propitiation."

---

[24] R. C. Sproul, *The Truth of the Cross* (Lake Mary, FL: Reformed Trust, 2007), 134.

Though a bit difficult, it's worth learning. It occurs four times in the Bible:

> God put forward [Jesus] as a propitiation by his blood, to be received by faith (Romans 3:25a).

> Therefore [Jesus] had to be made like his brothers in every respect, so that he might become a merciful and faithful high priest in the service of God, to make propitiation for the sins of the people (Hebrews 2:17).

> [Jesus] is the propitiation for our sins, and not for ours only but also for the sins of the whole world (1 John 2:2).

> In this is love, not that we have loved God but that he loved us and sent his Son to be the propitiation for our sins (1 John 4:10).

Propitiation means this—that *Jesus satisfied the wrath of God.* Sin demands punishment, and Jesus has met that demand in our place. Jesus drank the cup of the undiluted wrath of God, and He drained it, imbibing its very dregs (Matthew 26:39; John 18:11; Revelation 16:19b).

The Samaritan woman's sins weren't ignored by Jesus; they were paid for, in full. Jesus died for her immorality, her deception, her false religion. And He did the same for me.

I'm in no danger of God's wrath because Jesus exhausted it in my place when He died on the cross. My debt is *paid in full*—"finished" (John 19:30). My sins are *purged* in full (Hebrews 1:3). When it comes to me, *God is fresh out of wrath.* Jesus took it all in my place. There's no purgatory left for me— no hell left for me—no wrath left for me!

Jerry Bridges describes this concept as clearly as anyone I've encountered:

> I believe a word that forcefully captures the essence of Jesus' work of propitiation is the word *exhausted*. Jesus exhausted the wrath of God. It was not merely deflected and prevented from reaching us; it was exhausted. Jesus bore the full, unmitigated brunt of it. God's wrath against sin was unleashed in all its fury on His beloved Son. He held nothing back.[25]

Another helpful definition of propitiation comes from John Murray:

> The doctrine of the propitiation is precisely this: that God loved the objects of His wrath so much that He gave His own Son to the end that He by His blood should make provision for the removal of His wrath. It was Christ's so to deal with the wrath that the loved would no longer be the objects of wrath, and love would achieve its aim of making the children of wrath the children of God's good pleasure.[26]

This great truth has become the "soundtrack" of my life. I write about justification and propitiation more than any other theme—and it's not even close, as the hymn texts that close this chapter will demonstrate. There's a reason why I'm obsessed with the substitutionary atonement: It's the heart of the gospel, and the only hope of my soul!

---

[25] Jerry Bridges, *The Gospel for Real Life* (Colorado Springs, CO: NavPress, 2002), 54.
[26] John Murray, *The Atonement* (Philadelphia, PA: Presbyterian & Reformed, 1962), 36.

His Robes for Mine: The Great Exchange

By His life, Jesus provided us with a robe of righteousness. By His death, Jesus clothed Himself in our robe of unrighteousness. We are saved by Jesus' vicarious death and life. He traded places with us, "being made sin for us" so that we could "become the righteousness of God" through Him (2 Corinthians 5:21). One apt illustration of this exchange is Mark Twain's tale, *The Prince and the Pauper.* The two boys in the story look remarkably alike—a happy coincidence in many a novel! Wearied by their own redundant lives, they trade clothes. By doing so, they trade *destinies.* The pauper is treated as a prince, in spite of himself. The prince is treated as a pauper, in spite of his true identity, nearly being killed in the process.

In a true and infinitely more compelling exchange, Jesus has clothed us in His righteousness, and thereby given us His glorious standing with the Father. We are treated as beloved children, despite our sin. And Jesus has donned our unrighteousness, thereby taking the punishment it incurs. The Father *forsook* Him (Matthew 27:46), for iniquity separates sinners from God (Isaiah 59:2). The Father *crushed* Him, for sin requires God's wrath (Colossians 3:6). The Father *executed* Him, for the wages of sin is death (Romans 3:23).

So, the Samaritan woman, guilty as she was, was treated as though she were as righteous as Christ. Although I'm the chief of sinners, I'm treated as though I were as righteous as Christ. And although Christ is God's beloved, well-pleasing Son, He was treated as though He were God's enemy.

His robes for mine: such anguish none can know.
Christ, God's beloved, condemned as though His foe.
He, as though I, accursed and left alone;
I, as though He, embraced and welcomed home!

Christian, we are fond of saying that salvation is free. And so it is—to us! But it was infinitely costly to our Lord. Marvel at it. Weep at your sin, which required such an awful payment. Rejoice that God has provided such a great a salvation. And above all, worship!

Let me close this chapter by appealing to the reader who is not yet a Christian. You have had the gospel explained to you with great care and precision. You don't have to understand the entire Bible. But now you've been confronted with essential truths that can lead to your salvation.

You know that you're a sinner. You know that you can't earn the free gift of salvation. You know that Jesus was sent to earth on a rescue mission. You know He lived a perfect life. You know He died a dreadful death—in your place, paying the penalty for your sins.

Now, know this: Scripture says that if you will *repent of your sins and trust in Jesus Christ* as your only hope of salvation, you will be saved (Acts 3:19; 16:31). Don't overthink it. You're already lost. You're condemned. Jesus has done everything necessary for you to be forgiven.

Simply pray and receive the Lord Jesus Christ as your Savior. I'm begging you, and I pray that God is drawing you to Himself, even as you read. For Christ's sake, don't delay any longer! Trust Christ as the Savior of your soul.

"Gaze on the Christ"

Behold the Lamb, the spotless Lamb,
Who takes away our sin;
The debt we faced was not erased,
But paid in full by Him.

*Gaze on the Christ, our sacrifice
On altar made of wood.
Exalt the Lamb, the worthy Lamb,
Who bought us with His blood.*

"Salvation's Cup"

There was a cup of holy wrath
Which made our fearless Savior quake;
He prayed the cup from Him would pass,
Yet drank its dregs for sinners' sake.

"My Jesus, Fair"

My Jesus, fair, was pierced by thorns,
By thorns grown from the fall.
Thus He Who gave the curse was torn
To end that curse for all.

O love divine, O matchless grace—
That God should die for men!
With joyful grief I lift my praise,
Abhorring all my sin,
Adoring only Him.

My Jesus, meek, was scorned by men,
By men in blasphemy.
"Father, forgive their senseless sin!"
He prayed, for them, for me.

My Jesus, kind, was torn by nails,
By nails of cruel men.
And to His cross, as grace prevailed,
God pinned my wretched sin.

My Jesus, pure, was crushed by God,
By God, in judgment just.
The Father grieved, yet turned His rod
On Christ, made sin for us.

"His Robes for Mine"

His robes for mine: O wonderful exchange!
Clothed in my sin, Christ suffered 'neath God's rage.
Draped in His righteousness, I'm justified.
In Christ I live, for in my place He died.

I cling to Christ, and marvel at the cost:
Jesus forsaken, God estranged from God.
Bought by such love, my life is not my own.
My praise—my all—shall be for Christ alone.

His robes for mine: what cause have I for dread?
God's daunting Law Christ mastered in my stead.
Faultless I stand with righteous works not mine,
Saved by my Lord's vicarious death and life.

His robes for mine: God's justice is appeased.
Jesus is crushed, and thus the Father's pleased.
Christ drank God's wrath on sin, then cried, "'Tis done!"
Sin's wage is paid; propitiation won.

His robes for mine: such anguish none can know.
Christ, God's beloved, condemned as though His foe.
He, as though I, accursed and left alone;
I, as though He, embraced and welcomed home!

"Give Him Glory!"

Give glory to redemption's Lamb,
The Savior of the lost,
Who wore our flesh, then bore our curse
Upon a cruel cross.
He took the filth and guilt of sin;
He took the wrath it earned;
He reconciled our souls to God—
The wayward have returned!

We cry, "Glory! Honor! Blessing to the King!"
"Power! Splendor!" all creation sings;
We cry, "Wisdom! Riches! Thanks unto the Lamb!"
Endless praises to the great "I Am!"

"Jehovah's Bride"

We are His, a cherished bride,
Loved at such a lavish price—
Heaven's justice satisfied,
Paid by Heaven's sacrifice.
Who are we, to be adored
By the Lamb Who took our place?
Held by love's almighty cord,
We are His, a bride of grace.
We are His, a bride of grace.

PART
THREE

Jesus Satisfies Sinners

Jesus answered her, "If you knew the gift of God, and who it is that is saying to you, 'Give me a drink,' you would have asked him, and he would have given you living water." The woman said to him, "Sir, you have nothing to draw water with, and the well is deep. Where do you get that living water? Are you greater than our father Jacob? He gave us the well and drank from it himself, as did his sons and his livestock." Jesus said to her, "Everyone who drinks of this water will be thirsty again, but whoever drinks of the water that I will give him will never be thirsty again. The water that I will give him will become in him a spring of water welling up to eternal life." The woman said to him, "Sir, give me this water, so that I will not be thirsty or have to come here to draw water." Jesus said to her, "Go, call your husband, and come here." The woman answered him, "I have no husband." Jesus said to her, "You are right in saying, 'I have no husband'; for you have had five husbands, and the one you now have is not your husband. What you have said is true."

JOHN 4:10-18

5

DIRTY OR THIRSTY?

JOHN 4:16-18

*It has pleased God lately to teach me more than ever that [He] Himself
is the fountain of happiness; that likeness to him, friendship for him,
and communion with him, form the basis of all true enjoyment.*

SAMUEL PEARCE[27]

If you're like me, you probably think you know the Samaritan woman. For years I thought of the Samaritan woman as a first-century Elizabeth Taylor. I pictured her as a "cougar," a flirtatious woman who prowled for men, entering and exiting marriages at her pleasure, leaving a path of despondent men in her wake. Indomitable. Reckless. Carefree. Easy.

I was wrong.

Think through her conversation with Jesus again. Set aside your preconceptions. Focus. Have you noticed what Jesus indicated was the woman's primary need? He doesn't describe her as *dirty*, though He could. It certainly would have worked

---

[27] Samuel Pearce was an early supporter of modern missions. His enjoyment of God motivated him to seek the same for others through aggressive gospel advance. This quotation is cited by Tom Wells in *A Vision for Missions* (Carlisle, PA: Banner of Truth, 2003), 153.

with the water illustration: *"Ask of me, and I will give you water that can make you deep-down clean."* We know the woman was sinful. She—like everyone before and after her, including us—was morally filthy.

But Jesus doesn't offer to *cleanse her spiritual dirt.* He doesn't tell her she needs to be born again. Instead, He offers to *quench her spiritual thirst.*

That's huge. It gives us insight into the kind of person she was. It sheds light on her history and her character. She's not a woman to be scorned. She's a woman to be pitied—one of the saddest characters in Scripture. Her story breaks my heart.

British pastor G. Campbell Morgan wrote movingly about the woman's thirst and her interest in Jesus' living water: "'Give me this water, that I thirst not,' was the sigh, the sob of a discontented, disappointed, thirsty woman."[28] I'm certain that's true.

She had experienced repeated divorces.

In a previous chapter we noted that women were treated like property during the time of Christ. A man didn't speak to his wife in public. He didn't walk with her, but insisted on her following obediently behind him in a show of inferiority and submission. Remember this as we consider the woman's many divorces.

In one of the Pharisees' attempts to trap Jesus, they asked Him if it was lawful for a man to divorce his wife "for any cause" (Matthew 19:3). The respected rabbi Hillel, who was

[28] G. Campbell Morgan, *The Gospel According to John* (Grand Rapids, MI: Fleming Revell, 1992), 75.

alive during Jesus' boyhood, allowed divorce for the most petty reasons—even the wife's burning a meal or the husband's finding a more attractive woman. Pharisees, whom we often consider to be so very pious, taught that a man could cast off his bride on a whim. The famous Jewish historian Josephus, who divorced his own wife, tells how divorce was the prerogative of men:

> He who for any reason whatsoever (and many such causes happen to men) wishes to be separated from a wife who lives with him, must give it to her in writing that he will cohabit with her no longer, and by this means she shall have liberty to marry another man; but before this is done it is not permitted her to do so.[29]

Jesus defended marriage and women with His answer to the Pharisees' question (Matthew 19:1-12), limiting lawful divorce to situations where there has been immorality. But you'll notice that the Pharisees never asked Jesus if a *woman* could divorce her *husband*. Such a question would have been ludicrous—it just didn't happen. No woman in Judea or Samaria had the right to shame her husband by divorcing him. Divorce was a one-way street. The husband could give his wife a divorce certificate willy-nilly, at his pleasure. That wasn't the Law of God, but it was the law of the day. But women? They didn't divorce—they *were divorced.*

How does this affect our understanding of John 4? Well, the woman at the well isn't an Elizabeth Taylor. She hasn't left

---

[29] Flavius Josephus, *Antiquities*, 4.8.23.

her men. She's been kicked to the curb. Repeatedly. Mercilessly. Excruciatingly.

She had endured repeated disappointments.

So what was this woman after? Why did she keep taking chances? Let me tell you this: *It wasn't sex.* It's actually something very noble.

Imagine a young girl growing up in Sychar. What does she pretend? What does she aspire to? What does she dream of?

Well, what if I told you that all this woman really wanted was to get married, have a family, and live happily ever after? She wanted it *so badly.* She believed it would bring her life meaning. Fulfillment. Satisfaction. She longed to love and be loved in return. She *thirsted* for it.

Finally, she met her "Mr. Right." He proposed. She accepted. They married.

Only it didn't provide her the satisfaction she expected. She still felt empty inside, like something was missing. She was thirsty while she was married, but she was devastated when her husband kicked her to the curb like so much rubbish.

She was ashamed. Confused. And oh, *so thirsty!* But she still hoped.

Husband #2 came along. Maybe this was what she longed for. She married, longing to find meaning for her life. And like the first, he rejected her. He kicked her to the curb.

More thirsty than ever, she tried again. And again. And again. Each time her hopes were dashed. Each time her heart was broken. Each time the thirst of her soul grew more and more desperate.

I can't speak of it with dry eyes. Her story is terrible. It makes me weep.

A sixth man scoffs at the idea of marriage. *"I'm not making you my wife. I'm no fool. But I'll give you a house and a bed."* Imagine the hollowness of her eyes and numbness of her heart as she tries yet again, so desperate for the satisfaction that mercilessly eludes her. Or worse, maybe she's stopped hoping altogether. Maybe she's just going through the motions, emotionally dead even as she trudges aimlessly through her wretched life.

Perhaps the details aren't precisely as I've described them. But this much should be clear from what we know of her history and the way Christ addresses her need: *This isn't a prostitute.* It's a woman who from childhood dreamed of having a family. Just like my little girls.

Aside: A Word for Parents

Indulge the dad in me to take a brief detour.

Let me caution parents against making marriage and childbearing *the* goal of your children's lives—and especially your daughters' lives. I'm not telling you to promote secular feminism as opposed to biblical values. But teach your daughters that their value doesn't rest in their marital status.

Singleness isn't a trap from which to escape. Perhaps the Lord will allow them to marry. And perhaps He won't. But don't set them up for disappointment by making the rest of life a dress rehearsal for their wedding day. Such thinking parades as though it were conservative and virtuous, but it arises more from Disney cartoons than biblical teaching.

Teach your girls to find their fulfillment in *God*—whether single or married. Teach them to think. Teach them to achieve. Teach them to glorify God by maximizing whatever gifts they possess.

If God has a husband and children in their future, wonderful! Teach them to embrace their God-given roles as wife and mother. But please, *please* don't teach them that anything else is failure. Defining success and satisfaction in terms of family can have harrowing effects. Let the story of the Samaritan woman—who was once a wide-eyed little girl—teach you a valuable lesson!

The Anguish of a Parched Soul

Jesus meets this woman. He knows her story. He sees her heart. And He offers to quench the thirst of her heart. Yes, she's immoral. Yes, she's guilty. But what draws His attention and compassion is her tragic story and the spiritual thirst that drove it. He sees a broken reed and a smoking wick, and the sight inspires His pity (Isaiah 42:3; Matthew 12:20).

No soul is too small for His mercy;
No sin is too great for His grace!

Why does this move me? Because *I'm a Samaritan woman*. My soul thirsts for meaning and significance, too. So does yours. Everyone's does.

Our Samaritan friend thought a spouse would bring her life meaning. Certainly there are readers who feel the same. Let me tell you, marriage is great. But it won't satisfy your soul. My wife Lori is a great wife—but she's a bad god. Many marriages are a wreck for this very reason: the wife looks to the husband, or the husband to the wife, as the source of soul satisfaction. That's above your spouse's paygrade! You need to lower your expectations. Romance was never intended to satisfy your soul, contrary to the love songs on your playlist.

Others assume that having children will give their life ultimate meaning. That makes me smile. Kids are great. The best thing ever. But leaning on them to make you happy is folly. They're not gods, either, although giving them the power to crush your soul will certainly make them think they are. Enjoy them—but don't look to them for the meaning of life.

Others look to work. Or education. Or money. Or adventure. When all those *amoral* things fail to deliver, people move on to *immoral* things: pornography, or alcohol, or drugs, or an affair. Why? Because people are so very, very *thirsty*. It's the chronic spiritual condition of humanity. We're surrounded by people who are going round and round through the vanity cycle. They're confused, and dizzy, and empty!

Jesus' statement that those who drink what the world offers will thirst again (John 4:13) is true of more than just the water from Jacob's well:

- *"Whoever gets this job will still be thirsty."*
- *"Whoever takes this vacation will still be thirsty."*
- *"Whoever accomplishes this goal will still be thirsty."*
- *"Whoever views this pornography will still be thirsty."*
- *"Whoever drinks this cocktail will still be thirsty."*

Some 1000 years before Jesus' encounter with the woman at the well, King Solomon wrote on this same theme in the book of Ecclesiastes. For twelve chapters, the aged Solomon looked back on his life with regret. He talked about the sorrows and travail of life "under the sun" (used 28 times the book). He found life, with its promises and goals, its disappointments and successes, to be "vanity" (used 31 times in the book). Solomon was thirsty—so thirsty he envied a stillborn (Ecclesiastes 6:3)! As a noted theologian put it in the 1960s, *"I can't get no satisfaction."*

Solomon's thirst wasn't for lack of effort. He tried all the things we've already discussed. And he had the means to try them like nobody before or after him could. Think of it:

- If Solomon, the wisest man in history, couldn't find satisfaction in his education or work, do you think you will?
- If Solomon, with his world-renowned wealth, couldn't find satisfaction in his possessions, do you think you will?
- If Solomon, with his 700 wives and 300 concubines couldn't find satisfaction in marriage, or family, or just plain sensuality, do you think you will?
- If Solomon, with all his toys and adventures, couldn't find satisfaction in the "have a blast while you last" mantra of hedonism, do you think you will?

Learn from the regrets of sorrowful King Solomon—a fellow Samaritan woman! Attempting to find satisfaction in anything on earth will lead you to disappointment, destruction, and even damnation. Only Christ can satisfy your parched soul!

"Christ is Sufficient"

Nothing I've done could merit God's grace;
Nothing I'll do can take it away.
I have one hope, in life and death:
I have been clothed in Christ's righteousness.

Christ is sufficient! His work is finished!
He is my faith's Author and End;
Christ is enough—my Savior and Friend!

Nothing remains since Jesus has died;
Justice was paid; the Judge satisfied.
Great is my sin; greater His love;
I have been cleansed with Calvary's blood!

Nothing I've sought on earth satisfies;
I was designed to thirst after Christ.
Beckoned by Him, "Drink and be filled."
I am content, yet yearn for Him still.

Nothing but Christ can undo the Fall.
He will return to reign over all.
Come to us, Lord; right ev'ry wrong;
Soon the redeemed will join heaven's song.

6

NEVER THIRST AGAIN

JOHN 4:14

There is no heart satisfaction in this world, until we believe on Christ.
Jesus alone can fill up the empty places of our inward man.

J. C. RYLE[30]

God has so built man that apart from a personal knowledge
of the living God…everything else would be vapid.

WALTER C. KAISER, JR.[31]

My nephew Jonathan is a delight to me. He's seventeen, and he has Down Syndrome. We've been close for years, though he did find my big sneezes terrifying when he was young. For his first few years of life, he used sign language rather than speaking. The sign he used to indicate me—Uncle Chris— was to put his hands up to his nose and make a blowing sound. Ah, the joys of allergies! He had other signs he'd use at the table, like "please" and "thank you" and "more," which he'd

[30] Ryle, *Expository Thoughts*, 204.
[31] Walter C. Kaiser, *Toward an Old Testament Theology* (Grand Rapids, MI: Zondervan, 1978), 170.

sign by bunching the fingers on each of his hands and tapping them together.

When Jonathan was around four years old we were vacationing in Ocean City, NJ. On the boardwalk there was a giant slide—one of those where you sit on a pad and race down three small hills.

Well, "small" is a relative term. I offered to take Jonathan on the ride, and he agreed, though to a four-year-old the hill seemed impossibly high. The further we went up the stairs, the more nervous he got. He slowed his ascent, so I carried him. With each step he became a bit more tense in my arms, and he squeezed my neck a little tighter.

Eventually, it was our turn. I sat on the pad, and he sat on my lap—silent, stiff, and sullen. I hoped my nonchalance would communicate confidence. I used my best it-will-be-fine, isn't-this-fun, sing-songy voice. Parents, you know what I mean. "*One! Two! Three!*" Down we flew, over one hill, then another, then another. I didn't hear a peep. I'm not sure he even breathed. The rest of our family said his eyes were like saucers. He was completely terrified.

We stopped, and I waited for a shiver or a scream—anything to indicate that he was still conscious. What I didn't expect is the very thing that happened: he eagerly tapped his bunched fingers together. "*More!*"

Chuck Swindoll notes that "More!" is the heart cry of the thirsty people all around us:

> Have you noticed? A man never earns enough. A woman is never beautiful enough. Clothes are never fashionable

enough. Cars are never nice enough. Gadgets are never modern enough. Houses are never furnished enough. Food is never fancy enough. Relationships are never romantic enough. Life is never full enough.[32]

Broken Cisterns

The unending search for "more" is exhausting. Like the Samaritan woman and like Solomon, the hearts of our friends and neighbors are empty. Life feels pointless. They're thirsty. Their lives are train wrecks as they "look for love in all the wrong places."

When Jesus used the analogy of a thirsty heart in John 4, He was alluding to several Old Testament Scriptures which use the same imagery. Consider Jeremiah 2:13, where Jehovah indicts the people of Israel:

> My people have committed two evils: they have forsaken me, the fountain of living waters, and hewed out cisterns for themselves, broken cisterns that can hold no water.

Looking for satisfaction outside of God isn't just dumb—it's wicked. It's idolatry. When Paul says that "*covetousness...is idolatry*" in Colossians 3:5, the Greek word translated *covetousness* is *pleonexia*, which literally means "the need to have more."

The Samaritan woman's "broken cistern" was a husband. But her dream "held no water." Solomon's broken cisterns were many, but none brought satisfaction. He spends twelve

---

chapters of Ecclesiastes setting up the "punchline" of Ecclesiastes 12:13. The "end of the matter" or "moral of the story" is this: "Fear God and keep his commandments, for this is the whole duty of man."[33]

Only knowing and obeying God matters! Everything else will be a distraction—a broken cistern—until you find fulfillment in knowing God.

Contrast the countless broken cisterns of the world with the gracious provision of Jehovah described in Jeremiah 2:13. He calls Himself "the fountain of living waters." Sound familiar? Jesus offered to give the Samaritan woman "living water" (John 4:10). He promised her that she would "never be thirsty again" (John 4:14a). He promised that the water He could give would "become in [her] a spring of water welling up to eternal life" (John 4:14b).

What an amazing set of promises! Jesus doesn't describe salvation as something future, but present. We often conceive of the benefits of the gospel as though they are all reserved for "the sweet by and by." Heaven will be awesome, to be sure. Contrary to Joel Osteen, our *Best Life* isn't *Now*. That's only true of unbelievers, and it's something to lament, not celebrate. For hell-bound sinners, this is as good as it gets. But for the Christian, the best is yet to come!

Still, we do indeed enjoy many benefits of salvation today. Jesus satisfies us now. He doesn't promise riches or success or health. He says that His blessings are "in us"—internal (v. 14).

---

[33] The word "duty" is supplied by the translators in Ecclesiastes 12:13. The intent was to smooth out the Hebrew concept. However, Solomon isn't describing man's duty. Better, fearing and obeying God is "the whole of man." That's what life is about!

He gives joy, peace, purpose, and abundant life. It starts now, and it never ends. What great words for a thirsty world!

Isaiah 55:1-4 uses language much like Jeremiah 2:13, though the tone differs. Isaiah offers an invitation rather than a rebuke:

> Come, everyone who thirsts, come to the waters; and he who has no money, come, buy and eat! Come, buy wine and milk without money and without price. Why do you spend your money for that which is not bread, and your labor for that which does not satisfy? Listen diligently to me, and eat what is good, and delight yourselves in rich food. Incline your ear, and come to me; hear, that your soul may live; and I will make with you an everlasting covenant, my steadfast, sure love for David. Behold, I made him a witness to the peoples, a leader and commander for the peoples.

In the midst of His offer of bountiful spiritual blessings, Jehovah offers a lament for those who invest their lives foolishly, exhausting themselves and their resources for "that which does not satisfy" (v. 2). Once again, our Lord offers us free and lavish satisfaction (v. 1). This time, water is replaced by wine, milk, bread, and rich food, but the point is the same. And notice that those promises are rooted in the coming Messiah—the Son of David Who would be a worldwide leader, not only for Israel but for "the peoples" (vv. 3-4). The connections to John 4 are clear and powerful. Only Jesus, the Messiah, can satisfy! And He offers more than provision: "Delight yourselves" (v. 2)!

Proverbs 9 similarly contrasts the false promises of the world (personified as a seductress named Folly) with the bountiful provisions of Wisdom (personified as a lavish hostess). The two hostesses appeal to the simpleton with an almost identical offer (vv. 4, 16): "Turn in here!" Both offer satisfaction. But only Wisdom delivers on her promise. Folly leaves the simpleton thirsty—and ultimately takes his life.

Jesus Satisfies My Longings

With an eye on Jeremiah 2, Isaiah 55, Proverbs 9—and other texts such as Isaiah 12:3 and Psalms 36:9, 42:1-2, 63:1, and 143:6—Jesus makes the audacious claim to be the Giver of "living water." It's nothing less than a claim to deity: Jesus asserts that He can give what only God can give!

What Jesus offered to the Samaritan woman in a private conversation He offered on another occasion to a multitude of people gathered in Jerusalem for the Feast of Tabernacles. Take a look at John 7:37-39:

> On the last day of the feast, the great day, Jesus stood up and cried out, "If anyone thirsts, let him come to me and drink. Whoever believes in me, as the Scripture has said, 'Out of his heart will flow rivers of living water.'" Now this he said about the Spirit, whom those who believed in him were to receive, for as yet the Spirit had not been given, because Jesus was not yet glorified.

At the beginning of John 4 we see Jesus avoiding a scrape with the Jewish leaders. In John 7, He provokes them, or at least risks provoking them. Jerusalem is teeming with people, as Jews had made one of their mandatory pilgrimages to the city for the Feast. "On the last day of the feast" there was a "solemn assembly" (Leviticus 23:36). At its climax there was a symbolic pouring out of water, representing Jehovah's wondrous provision for the Israelites when He brought forth water from the rock (Exodus 17:1-7; 1 Corinthians 10:4).

At that strategic, sacred time, Jesus demands the attention of the multitudes with a cry. Unlike the typical rabbi, He stands, claiming the role of a herald making a pronouncement. And He invites the people—whom dead religion has left spiritually parched—to drink deeply of the soul-satisfying water only *He* could provide.

With this appeal, Jesus tacitly but clearly claims to be Jehovah, the Giver of life-sustaining water! He claims to do what the religious leaders in Jerusalem could not. And as in John 4, He promises that the satisfaction will be uncontainable—the life of the indwelling Spirit will overflow and be obvious to others (4:14; 7:38-39). What an audacious offer! What an audacious claim!

Jesus satisfies. *Only* Jesus satisfies. And He satisfies us by giving us *Himself,* not some other gift. John Piper makes this helpful distinction: "The deepest and most enduring happiness is found only in God. Not from God, but in God."[34]

Augustine famously describes our thirst for Christ in this way:

> Thou hast made us for thyself, O Lord, and our hearts are restless until they find their rest in thee.[35]

---

[34] John Piper, *Desiring God* (Sisters, OR: Multnomah Publishers: 2003), 28.
[35] Augustine, *Confessions,* 1.1.1.

Yes, we are restless. Dissatisfied. Thirsty. And in His infinite grace and wisdom, God *intentionally* made us so we would be so! He has "put eternity into man's heart" (Ecclesiastes 3:11). Our dissatisfaction with life isn't accidental; it has a divine intent: to drive us to God, the only Source of true joy! Our spiritual thirst is a God-ordained magnet He uses to draw us to Himself. Walter C. Kaiser, Jr. acknowledges this ingenious design:

> God has so built man that apart from a personal knowledge of the living God...everything else would be vapid.[36]

Doesn't that describe the people around you? Aren't their lives empty? Aren't they frustrated? Aren't they thirsty? Don't they need to hear of the satisfying work of Jesus? Don't you need to tell them?

I'm a music lover. I thank God for a rich heritage of psalms, hymns, and spiritual songs. There are many Christian songs that elaborate on the theme of the soul's satisfaction in Christ.

Joseph Hart echoes Jesus' invitation in "Come Ye Sinners, Poor and Needy":

> *Come, ye thirsty, come, and welcome,*
> *God's free bounty glorify;*
> *True belief and true repentance,*
> *Every grace that brings you nigh.*

Richard E. Blanchard, Sr. based an entire song on the woman at the well in "Fill My Cup, Lord":

---

[36] Kaiser, *Toward an Old Testament Theology,* 170.

Like the woman at the well, I was seeking
For things that could not satisfy.
And then I heard my Savior speaking—
"Draw from My well that never shall run dry."

Fill my cup, Lord; I lift it up, Lord;
Come and quench this thirsting of my soul.
Bread of Heaven, feed me till I want no more.
Fill my cup, fill it up and make me whole.

There are millions in this world who are seeking
For pleasures earthly things afford.
But none can match the wondrous treasure
That I find in Jesus Christ my Lord.

So my brother, if the things this world gave you
Leave hungers that won't pass away,
My blessed Lord will come and save you
If you kneel to Him and humbly pray.[37]

More simply, Jean S. Piggot writes of the Savior's ability to satisfy in "Jesus, I Am Resting, Resting":

Simply trusting Thee, Lord Jesus,
I behold Thee as Thou art,
And Thy love, so pure, so changeless,
Satisfies my heart;
Satisfies its deepest longings,
Meets, supplies its every need,
Compasseth me round with blessings:
Thine is love indeed!

Perhaps my favorite "satisfaction song," however, is simply called "Satisfied." I learned it as a child in Pueblo, Colorado, where my dad was a church planter. One of the men in our church was named Mr. Ingle. He was *old*—like a dinosaur to my boyish eyes. He was always at church, always wearing headphones in an only moderately successful attempt to hear, and always leaning *way* back with his knees on the pew in front of him in a futile attempt to get comfortable. But he was godly.

A few times I went along when my dad visited Mr. Ingle in an apartment that seemed to me like a cell. It was tight. It was dark. It was sad, in a way. But it was filled with the aroma of Christ. This man loved the Word of God.

As a result, Mr. Ingle also loved the souls of men. He would often walk from his home to the Pueblo bus station. I went with him a few times, and bus stations were even more sketchy in the 1970s than they are today, if that's possible. He went to the bus station not to catch a bus but to find weary and bored travelers. His sole intent was to give them the gospel. He'd met Jesus, and he was desperate that others should know Jesus, too.

Mr. Ingle was old. Eccentric. And one of the most passionate evangelists I've ever known.

Each time our church allowed members to request a hymn, Mr. Ingle would ask us to sing Clara T. Williams' beautiful song, "Satisfied." It mingles the story of the woman at the well and the story of the prodigal son. I'm certain he thought of the song as his spiritual biography. It meant so much to him, and it consequently means a great deal to me. Mr. Ingle left his mark on me. Even now, I write of him through tears. Here's the text he so loved:

All my life long I had panted
For a drink from some cool spring,
That I hoped would quench the burning
Of the thirst I felt within.

Hallelujah! I have found Him
Whom my soul so long has craved!
Jesus satisfies my longings;
Through His blood I now am saved.

Feeding on the husks around me,
Till my strength was almost gone,
Longed my soul for something better,
Only still to hunger on.

Poor I was, and sought for riches,
Something that would satisfy,
But the dust I gathered round me
Only mocked my soul's sad cry.

Well of water, ever springing,
Bread of life, so rich and free,
Untold wealth that never faileth,
My Redeemer is to me.

The only adaptation I would make to this lovely song is this:

Hallelujah! *He* has found *me!*

Is it not so? Isn't that the point of John 4? Of your life? Jesus seeks sinners. And saves them. And *satisfies* them. *Hallelujah!*

Four Applications

Let me close this portion of the book with four applications which I pray will "leave their mark" on your soul, much as Mr. Ingle forever influenced mine.

First, let the "satisfaction" facet of Jesus' saving work alter your view of Christianity. It may be a Copernicus-like shift for many.

For years, I conceived of my Christian life as a *duty* rather than a *delight*. Perhaps due to preaching I heard, or just due to my inner legalist, I thought of Christianity as a sort of "straightjacket." There were sinful things I wished I could do. I dreaded missing out. I determined to try to avoid doing wrong but enjoyable things, motivated by duty.

But I didn't understand that what Jesus calls me to is infinitely superior to what the world offers! He calls me to abundant life, to delight, to joy. And unlike the siren calls of the world, He actually delivers! As in Psalm 1, He promises a life that is analogous to a lush, healthy, fruit-bearing tree—so unlike the "chaff-like" life the world gives.

Analogies like that are all over Scripture. God calls you to joy! As John Piper has so helpfully taught me and countless others, "God is most glorified in us when we are most satisfied in Him."[38] Amen!

Second, apply Jesus' power to satisfy to your struggles with temptation.

Believe this to be true: *There is more satisfaction in Jesus than in sin!* I emphasized this point repeatedly to Tracy,

---

[38] This is the theme of John Piper's ministry, Desiring God. It's unpacked in John Piper's book of the same name, *Desiring God*. I commend it to you.

a dear lady I pastored in Ohio. Despite her church attendance, steady job, and seemingly happy family, Tracy was an alcoholic. She'd had a DUI in her past. She'd been through programs like Alcoholics Anonymous. I'm grateful for the compassion of that organization. It's helped many who are bound with addictions. Unfortunately, it didn't help Tracy.

Tracy came to me at wit's end. I knew her problem was beyond my paygrade, so I sent her to the wisest man ever to live: I assigned her to study Ecclesiastes. She listed the things Solomon used to fill the void in his heart. She noted that it was all vain. And she learned that what she was missing was a deep, satisfying relationship with God.

I'll never forget the day she called me from her car, choking back tears. She told me how she'd just come out of the grocery store. Like countless other times, she had stood in the beer aisle. Like countless other times, a battle had raged. But unlike other times, she had emerged triumphant. *"Pastor, I said it right out loud: 'There is more satisfaction in Jesus than in this stupid beer.' And I left the store—without the beer!"*

I love the way John Piper describes the temptation-defeating power of finding our satisfaction in Christ:

> I know of no other way to triumph over sin long-term than to gain a distaste for it because of a superior satisfaction in God.[39]

This is a life-changing truth. Jesus is better than alcohol, or pornography, or sex, or money, or food. Believe it!

---

[39] Piper, *Desiring God*, 12.

Third, believe that God wants you to enjoy your life.

While life apart from Christ is empty, life *with* Christ is full of joy. Life doesn't have to be "vain." As we've noted, your spouse can't satisfy your soul. But once you find ultimate satisfaction in your walk with Christ, you can really enjoy your marriage, sans the pressure you had placed on your spouse to be your god.

Many of the things Solomon found to be vain are actually good gifts of God once you stop treating them as idols. He says as much in Ecclesiastes (2:24-25; 3:11-13, 22; 11:9-10). So, find your satisfaction in Jesus—*then* enjoy your family, your career, your vacations, and the rest of your life. Excel at work. Cross things off your bucket list. Enjoy art, and music, and movies, and great books. They're great gifts, as long as you don't make them gods.

In the slightly altered words of Matthew 6:33, "Seek first the kingdom of God and His righteousness—then have a blast with the rest of the things God provides."

Finally, make it your life's ambition to share this good news with others.

Be another Mr. Ingle. Once you've been satisfied, live to tell others that they can be as soul-satisfied as you are.

Remember how we've seen the "satisfaction" theme all through Scripture—from Psalms, Proverbs, and Ecclesiastes; from Isaiah and Jeremiah; from John 4 and John 7? Well, there are two more invitations for thirsty sinners to come and drink of the waters of life.

The first comes in Revelation 21:6, where God repeats the promises made throughout both Testaments: "To the thirsty I

will give from the spring of the water of life without payment."
Again, He satisfies the thirsty. Again, the water is free.

The final invitation to thirsty sinners comes in Revelation
22, the very last chapter of the Bible. That's significant! God
and the redeemed call out together, urging Samaritan women
to find their satisfaction in Christ. Respond to the invitation
of Revelation 22:17—then spend your life *repeating* it:

> The Spirit and the Bride say, "Come." And let the one who
> hears say, "Come." And let the one who is thirsty come; let
> the one who desires take the water of life without price.

"Relentless Love"

Relentless love transforms my soul and its delights—
Exceeds the fleeting joys which once sufficed.
Held by His love for me—a hold which sets me free!—
I have my heart's desire, and that is Christ.

> *Unbounded love, unfailing love,*
> *Love raised upon a tree;*
> *Unending love, prevailing love—*
> *My Savior's sovereign love for me.*

"Salvation's Cup"

> *Our thirst is quenched by Christ the Lord,*
> *Who gives His cup and takes our own.*
> *We taste and see that He is good;*
> *He satisfies, and He alone!*

PART
FOUR

Jesus Turns Sinners into Worshipers

The woman said to him, "Sir, I perceive that you are a prophet. Our fathers worshiped on this mountain, but you say that in Jerusalem is the place where people ought to worship." Jesus said to her, "Woman, believe me, the hour is coming when neither on this mountain nor in Jerusalem will you worship the Father. You worship what you do not know; we worship what we know, for salvation is from the Jews. But the hour is coming, and is now here, when the true worshipers will worship the Father in spirit and truth, for the Father is seeking such people to worship him. God is spirit, and those who worship him must worship in spirit and truth.

JOHN 4:19-24

7

WORSHIP IN SPIRIT AND TRUTH

JOHN 4:19-24

We are brought to God and to faith and to salvation that we might worship and adore Him... God has provided His salvation that we might be, individually and personally, vibrant children of God, loving God with all our hearts and worshiping Him in the beauty of holiness.

We are saved to worship God. All that Christ has done for us in the past and all that He is doing now leads to this one end.

A. W. TOZER[40]

Jesus *seeks, saves,* and *satisfies* sinners. That's awesome. But then what? It's significant that God's interest in the Samaritan woman doesn't end at the point of her conversion. God saved her for a purpose. He saves all of us for a purpose. He has designs beyond rescuing us from hell, beyond securing us for heaven, beyond showing us compassion. *God saves sinners to turn them into worshipers.* This is evident from John 4 and from the rest of the Bible. Again, John 4 is a microcosm of what

---

[40] A. W. Tozer, *Whatever Happened to Worship? A Call to True Worship*, ed. Gerald B. Smith (Camp Hill, PA: Christian Publications, 1985), 14, 94.

God is doing in the world. God is seeking worshipers. That's the very agenda that brought Jesus to the well in the first place.

Worship Wars

John 4's beautiful discussion of worship begins with an evasive measure. Unmasked as a five-time divorcee and fornicator, the Samaritan woman is eager for a change of topic. *"Let's talk about something else—anything else!"* She brings up a theological controversy, hoping to remove attention from the skeletons Jesus has just dragged out of her closet and into the hot noontime sun.

She's neither the first nor the last person who would rather engage in a theological debate than grow in grace. It makes me wonder how much blustering about theological mysteries is merely the smoke and mirrors of a guilty conscience. At any rate, though her motives may be suspect, the woman brings up an important issue:

> Our fathers worshiped on this mountain, but you say that in Jerusalem is the place where people ought to worship (John 4:20).

We tend to think that worship wars are a new thing. In our day we've focused on the use or nonuse of drums. In Reformer John Calvin's day, he forbade the use of all musical instruments. (Strange, for a guy who loved the Psalms as much as Calvin did!) In Paul's day debate surrounded the observance of special days and the question of circumcision. During Jesus' ministry, He was often critiqued for His supposed abuse of the Sabbath. There is nothing new under the sun.

Sadly, many think the word *worship* is a "call to arms" rather than a "call to prayer." Think I'm exaggerating? Do a word search for "worship" on a sermon site, like Sermon-Audio.com. At least half of the messages will focus more on debate than doxology. That can't be a good thing.

The debate between the Jews and Samaritans focused on the location of proper worship. As we noted in chapter 2, following the division of Solomon's kingdom, King Jeroboam set up an idolatrous worship system in northern Israel to keep his subjects from making pilgrimages to Jerusalem in Judah (1 Kings 12:26-33). Although Jeroboam's people were Jews—ethnic Samaritans didn't exist for another 250 to 300 years—his actions set the tone for idolatry in the region.

Later, the ethnic Samaritans (formed by the mandatory mingling of conquered Jews with Gentiles; 2 Kings 17:23-24) went further in their false religion, actually altering Scriptures such as Deuteronomy 27:4 to point Samaritan worshipers to Mount Gerizim in Samaria rather than to the temple in Jerusalem. Tradition *trumped* and eventually *twisted* Scripture.

Notice the lady's source of authority: "Our fathers worshiped on this mountain" (v. 20). Tragically, multitudes of people are lost because they cling relentlessly to the religious ideals of their forebears. As J. C. Ryle puts it, "'Our fathers did so,' is one of the natural man's favorite arguments."[41]

Ironically, the temple in Jerusalem was glamorous while only ruins remained of the temple at Gerizim. Still, it wasn't clear to the woman who was right. So, she asks, and in

---

[41] Ryle, *Expository Thoughts,* 220.

another demonstration of condescending grace, Jesus conducts an impromptu seminar on worship. One of the most important lessons on worship in the entire Bible is given to an audience of one. Thankfully, we get to eavesdrop!

Salvation is from the Jews

Jesus' answer to the "where" question has three components to it.

First, He tells her that the shelf-life of the debate was short. The hour was approaching when worship would focus on *neither* location (v. 21). That's a stunning statement, coming from a Jew! It paves the way for an even more audacious statement in John 4:23. And it builds on a promise of universal worship in Malachi 1:11, which predicts a day when "in *every place* incense will be offered to [Jehovah's] name."

Before taking sides, Jesus indicates that the question itself is flawed, focusing on *where* worship should take place rather than *Whom* we should worship, and *how*. Again, it makes me wonder if one of the casualties of worship wars is worship itself.

Second, He tells the Samaritan woman that her people are on the wrong side of the debate: "You [Samaritans] worship what you do not know" (v. 22a). Jesus is gracious, but His kindness never displaces the truth. He tells her that she and the Samaritans are wrong because they are ignorant. They were idolaters. It wasn't a race issue. It was a truth issue. Truth matters, and worship without truth is idolatry. Even when the ignorance is unintentional, it is still inexcusable. Calvin comments that when Jesus condemns the Samaritans for ignorant worship, "all good intentions, as they are called, are struck by this sentence, as by a thunderbolt."[42] Unbiblical, uninformed worship is idolatry, no matter how sincere it may be.

Finally, Jesus sides with the Jews: "We [Jews] worship what we know, for salvation is from the Jews" (v. 22b). The short answer to her question is "Jerusalem." The Jews are right, not the Samaritans. In the Old Covenant, God established the true temple in Jerusalem, not Mount Gerizim (2 Chronicles 6:6; Psalm 48:1-2).

The irony is that Jesus was completely unimpressed with the state of Judaism in His day. He skewered the Pharisees for their hypocrisy, their lack of compassion, and their ignorance of the Scriptures. In fact, Jesus often looked to Gentiles to find genuine, audacious faith (Matthew 8:10).

Jesus was also unimpressed by the Jerusalem temple. He corrected His disciples when they were awestruck by the glories of Herod's temple in Jerusalem (Mark 13:1)—in part, no doubt, because the lavish temple complex was a tribute to Herod the Great's tyrannical narcissism. After all, the Herod who built the temple complex and epic fortresses like Masada and the Herodian was the same ruler who slaughtered the innocents in Jerusalem in his bloodthirsty attempt to kill the infant Jesus (Matthew 2:16-18).

Despite the many abuses of Judaism in Jesus' day, He still explains to the Samaritan woman that "salvation is from the Jews" (John 4:22).[43] This is an affirmation of biblical truth,

---

[42] John Calvin, *Commentary on the Gospel according to John*, vol. 1 (Grand Rapids, MI: Baker Books, 1999), 159.

[43] Kenneth Bailey notes that Jesus' statement that "salvation is from the Jews" (not the Gentiles or Samaritans) demonstrates that John's Gospel isn't "anti-Semitic" as is often charged. *Jesus Through Middle Eastern Eyes*, 210.

not of the Pharisaism and dead legalism of His day. Don't confuse the two!

In what sense were the Jews the conduit for God's great work of salvation? First, the Jews were given the *Scriptures*. Second, the Jews were given the *worship system*, including the priesthood, sacrifices, and temple.

Most importantly, the Jews were given the *Messiah*. The promised Deliverer would come from the line of Eve (Genesis 3:15), of Abraham, Isaac, and Jacob (Genesis 18:18; 22:18; 26:4; 28:14), of Judah (Genesis 49:10), and ultimately of David (2 Samuel 7:12-13; Isaiah 9:7). The Messiah was a Jew—the very Jew Who was talking to the Samaritan at that moment! Salvation was held in trust by the Jews, not only for their good, but so that through the promised Messiah "all the nations of the earth [would] be blessed" (Genesis 22:18).

Worship in Spirit and Truth

What comes next in the story is probably a familiar text. Jesus uses the woman's question as a springboard and launches into a vital discussion on the topic of worship. In John 4:23-24 Jesus gives us essential instructions regarding the nature of worship—and indeed, regarding the nature of God Himself:

> But the hour is coming, and is now here, when the true worshipers will worship the Father in spirit and truth, for the Father is seeking such people to worship him. God is spirit, and those who worship him must worship in spirit and truth (John 4:23-24).

First, worship must be in *spirit*. In my opinion, this is best understood not as a reference to the Holy Spirit, but to the spirit of the worshiper. A definite article is typically used in the Gospel of John when the Holy Spirit is in view—"*the* Spirit." But both verses 23 and 24 omit the article. Jesus is speaking of worship in spirit, not in *the* Spirit.

What this means is that worship is a matter of the heart, not mere externals. Jesus is insisting upon worship *from the heart* as opposed to worship *by external places, objects, and rituals.* It was possible for Jews in the Old Testament and in Jesus' day to draw near to God with their lips while their hearts were far from Him (Isaiah 29:13; Matthew 15:8-9). It was possible for Pharisees to go through the motions of worship—saying prayers, giving alms, and fasting—in an exhibition before men rather than in genuine, heartfelt worship (Matthew 6:1-18).

The Pharisees didn't have a corner on religious formalism. It is just as possible in our day to attend church, bow in prayer, sing a song, and give an offering—and to do it all without worshiping. "Playing church" doesn't honor God. On the contrary, it offends Him. He would rather have no worship at all than bogus worship (Isaiah 1:11-15; 66:3; Psalm 51:16-17). To go through forms of worship without true adoration is to take God's name in vain (Exodus 20:7). Scripture requires worship in spirit.

The Bible requires spiritual worship specifically because "*God* is spirit" (John 4:24). Worship must be consistent with the God to Whom it is offered. Because God is spiritual, not physical, *worship* must be spiritual, not physical. Matthew

Henry explains this clearly and succinctly: "The spirituality of the divine nature is a very good reason for the spirituality of divine worship."[44] We must align the character of our worship with the character of our God.

That's not to say that externals are irrelevant when it comes to worship. The very God Who must be worshiped "in spirit" also gave His people meticulous details in the Law about *how* to worship Him. He didn't say that all forms of worship are legitimate "as long as your heart is in the right place." Not at all! Externals *do* matter; they're just not a *substitute* for internals.

Of course, worship that originates in our spirit will affect our entire being. The book of Psalms—what Michael Barrett helpfully describes as our "hymnbook" and "handbook" for worship[45]—describes worship that *moves* us. It *affects* us. And we *express* it in a variety of ways. Weeping (39:12). Bowing down (95:6). Singing (7:17). Shouting (33:1, 3). Clapping (47:1). Lifting hands (63:4). Dancing (150:4).

Are all of those biblical expressions of praise exercised in your public worship service? Probably not. Should they be? Not necessarily. Perhaps we can dismiss some of the expressions as being tied to the culture of the day. But we should ask ourselves why worship in the Psalms is so very *expressive* and worship in many churches today is so very *stoic*. What exactly *does* fervent worship look like in our day? It's a question worth asking.

---

[44] Matthew Henry, *Matthew Henry's Commentary on the Whole Bible* (Peabody, MA: Hendrickson, 1995), 1937.
[45] Michael P. V. Barrett, *The Beauty of Holiness* (Greenville, SC: Ambassador-Emerald International, 2006), 175.

Shortly after I preached on expressions of worship from the Psalms at Killian Hill Baptist Church, Brenda—a founding member who is in her 70s—came to me with a confession:

> Pastor, I was so moved when we sang "Before the Throne of God Above" at the end of this morning's service that I *tried* to raise my hands. I really did. *But they just wouldn't go up!*

We both laughed. I told her not to pull a muscle. I was pleased that her heart was moved. She was welcome to keep her hands safely at her sides.

Worship must be "in spirit." That's essential. But it's not sufficient. There's more.

Jesus also teaches that worship must be *in truth*. As opposed to what? Well, as opposed to error. As opposed to human innovations. Worship rests in the truth of God's Word. We don't worship according to manmade tradition (like the Samaritans) or our own preferences (like Cain and countless others). We worship God as Scripture dictates. Indeed, the Bible should fill our worship services:

- We *read* the Word, giving the public reading of Scripture a prominent place in our corporate worship (1 Timothy 4:13).[46]

- We *pray* the Word, aligning our prayers with the prayers of Scripture and the will of God revealed in Scripture (1 John 5:14).

---

[46] I will often read a large portion of Scripture to begin my message in addition to the regular Scripture reading that begins our service. My reasoning? It's the only part of the sermon that I'm positive I'm getting right!

- We *sing* the Word, both by singing the Psalms and by singing songs that are saturated with Scripture (Colossians 3:16).

- We *preach* the Word, recognizing that preaching is at the heart of worship; it has as much to do with exaltation as with edification and evangelism (2 Timothy 4:2).

- We *support* and *submit to* the Word through our financial offerings (Galatians 6:6).

- We *picture* the Word, tying both the ordinance of baptism and the ordinance of the Lord's Table to their doctrinal, gospel-centered roots (Matthew 28:18-20; 1 Corinthians 11:23-34).

Calvin concludes that "if we wish our religion to be approved by God, it must rest on knowledge obtained from His word."[47]

Worship in truth is *biblical* worship. It's rooted in the Word of God, not the whims of man. And it's legitimate worship, not contrived. It's true, as opposed to *fake*. It's sincere. (This obviously overlaps with the concept of worship in spirit, which we've already addressed.)

Worship through Christ

Here's the thing: Everything I've said about worship in spirit and truth was true in the Old Testament. God has *always* required worship that is both Scriptural and spiritual. Right? *Right?*

---

[47] Calvin, *Commentary on the Gospel according to John,* 161.

And that means we haven't correctly understood the text yet. I've heard John 4:23-24 preached countless times describing worship which Moses, David, and Elijah would have experienced. But we're not reading a description of acceptable worship from the Pentateuch. We're not reading from the Minor Prophets. We're in John 4, and Jesus is telling us that worship in spirit and in truth is a *new* thing—a *revolutionary* thing! Remember His momentous statement before He spoke about worship in spirit and truth? Read it again.

First, in verse 21, He says that "the hour is coming" when worship would be freed from either Jerusalem or Gerizim. That's exciting.

But then in verse 23 He says that "the hour is coming, *and is now here,* when true worshipers will worship in spirit and in truth." This is a stupendous statement! The hour *had arrived* when worship fundamentally changed. Why? Because *Jesus* had arrived!

So, no one had ever worshiped God "in spirit and in truth" as Jesus conceived of it before Jesus' arrival. Moses hadn't. David hadn't. Elijah hadn't. Jesus isn't merely restating the Old Testament's calls for Scriptural and spiritual worship. He's saying that the very basis and nature of worship has changed because of His arrival.

If we miss this, we're missing the genius of John 4:23-24. Indeed, we're missing the genius of Christianity. God accepts our worship not because "we're doing it right" but because of our association with Jesus. Just as the mythical character Rumpelstiltskin could turn worthless straw into priceless gold, Jesus takes our straw-like offerings and transforms them into worship that God not only receives, but delights in! That's the point of Hebrews 13:15:

> Through him [Jesus] then let us continually offer up a sacrifice of praise to God, that is, the fruit of lips that acknowledge his name.

The worship which God accepts today isn't tied to a location, whether that location is Jerusalem or the building where your local church meets. The worship God accepts today isn't just heartfelt. It isn't even just Scriptural. *The worship God accepts today is Christ-centered! It depends on Jesus, just as every other part of our relationship with God depends on Jesus.* That's the ultimate meaning of John 4:23-24. The topic of these classic verses isn't the form of worship. Mercy, that's exactly what Jesus is *undoing* in His conversation with this woman.

Jesus is the focus of worship that is "in spirit and in truth." The world-changing truth that worship is based on the person and work of Christ is a grand theme that deserves more attention, so we'll return to it in the next chapter. For now, understand this: the redeemed people who lived before Jesus worshipped God truly and sincerely, but they never worshiped God in spirit and in truth as Jesus described. That privilege belongs to those blessed to live after Jesus' arrival—including the Samaritan woman.

God is Seeking Worshipers

I'll close this chapter by highlighting the second half of John 4:23: "The Father is seeking such people to worship Him."

That's an amazing statement, and it ties together seemingly disjointed portions of John 4. Remember how we learned that Jesus pursues sinners? That He seeks and saves the lost (Luke 19:10)? Well, here's the reason! Jesus is seeking *sinners* because God is seeking *worshipers*. It's the same pursuit! It's one thing, not two. And it's all part of God's great masterplan. A. W. Tozer describes the *totality* of Jesus' ministry as a search for worshipers:

> Jesus was born of a virgin, suffered under Pontius Pilate, died on the cross and rose from the grave to make worshipers out of rebels![48]

Gathering worshipers was Jesus' mission. And gathering worshipers is the *church's* mission. That's why John Piper's memorable statement regarding the doxological purpose of evangelism is so profoundly correct: "Missions exist because worship doesn't."[49]

Worship is the ultimate goal of redemption. When God told Pharaoh to let His people go so that they could worship Him (Exodus 5:1; 7:16; 8:1; et al.), it wasn't a ruse. God was telling Pharaoh—of all people—that the purpose of the exodus was God's glory. God was redeeming the enslaved children of Israel from Egypt because He was gathering worshipers! The goal of salvation is exaltation. I'm grateful to Ligon Duncan for pointing this out in an unforgettable sermon at the Together for the Gospel conference in 2006, and then publishing it in *Give Praise to God:*

---

[48] Tozer, *Whatever Happened to Worship*, 11.
[49] John Piper, *Let the Nations Be Glad! The Supremacy of God in Missions* (Grand Rapids, MI: Baker Academic, 2010), 15.

Do not underestimate this repeated language. This is not merely a ruse to get Pharaoh to temporarily release the children of Israel. It is the primary reason why God sets his people free: to worship Him. The primacy of worship in a believer's life is, thus, set forth. We are saved to worship![50]

With even greater clarity, Ephesians tells us again and again that salvation's end game is God's glory. Soteriology (the doctrine of salvation) yields doxology (the glory of God). Ephesians 1-3 unpack the treasure chest of salvation blessings which God has lavished on us, including election, adoption, redemption, and forgiveness. Why? For His own glory:

Ephesians 1:6 – *"To the praise of his glorious grace…"*

Ephesians 1:12 – *"So that we who were the first to hope in Christ might be to the praise of his glory."*

Ephesians 1:14 – *"…to the praise of his glory."*

Ephesians 2:7 – *"…so that in the coming ages he might show the immeasurable riches of his grace in kindness toward us in Christ Jesus."*

Ephesians 3:20-21 – *"Now to him who is able to do far more abundantly than all that we ask or think, according to the power at work within us, to him be glory in the church and in Christ Jesus throughout all generations, forever and ever. Amen."*

God's search for worshipers demonstrates the doxological purpose of all things. He is seeking His glory. But it also demonstrates the condescension and compassion of God. He is

---

[50] J. Ligon Duncan, "Does God Care How We Worship?" in *Give Praise to God,* eds. Philip Graham Ryken, Derek W. H. Thomas, and J. Ligon Duncan (Phillipsburg, NJ: Presbyterian & Reformed, 2003), 29.

dispensing grace even as He is collecting glory. The motive for God's grace is God's glory.

Once again, we see in John 4 a microcosm of what God is doing in the world. What's the Bible about? What's God up to? This! The whole biblical record has worship as the object of salvation! God *created* us to worship Him (Revelation 4:11). We violently rebelled against that purpose when we fell. So now, in His great grace, God is *re-creating* us to worship Him (Revelation 5:9-12). God is seeking worshipers.

God is Making Worshipers

There's just one problem: When God looks throughout the earth, He doesn't find a bunch of good-hearted people just waiting to be assembled into a heavenly choir. Rather, He finds rebels. He sees only our backs as we defiantly run our own way (Isaiah 53:6; Romans 3:10-11).

God is seeking worshipers. But He doesn't *find* them. He *makes them!*

From what? *From Samaritan women like us.* And He does so through the life-changing power of the gospel!

"Holy, Mighty, Worthy"

Copyright © 2006 churchworksmedia.com. All rights reserved.

"Glory, glory, glory!" We, Thy church, adore Thee.
Called by grace to bring Thee praise; trophies of Thy pow'r to save!
None shall share Thy glory! All shall bow before Thee.
Father, Son and Spirit: One! "Glory, glory, glory!"

8

JESUS, THE PERFECT TEMPLE

JOHN 4:23-24

*When Jesus told the woman that the Father was seeking true worshippers,
he was indicating that with his presence now on earth the age-old quest
for worshippers would be fulfilled in him and not on some mountain.
Jesus' mission was to bring people to the Father by faith in him (John
14:6-7). True worship is only in him because only he can provide eternal
life—only through him can anyone come to the Father.*

ALLEN P. ROSS[51]

Christ's announcement in John 4:23 changed worship forever.
It wasn't just a change of the proper *venue* of worship. It was
much, much more! Jesus' arrival changed the very *basis* and
nature of worship. Jesus made the entire worship system of the
Old Covenant obsolete.

He *is* the perfect Sacrifice.

He *is* the perfect High Priest.

And He *is* the perfect Temple.

---

[51] Allen P. Ross, *Recalling the Hope of Glory* (Grand Rapids, MI: Kregel, 2006), 385.

As marvelous as it is that Jesus is our sacrifice and high priest, it is Jesus' replacement of the temple that is the focus of John 4. For that reason, it will also be the focus of this chapter.

Let's consider how Jesus related to the Jerusalem temple during His time on earth.

Jesus Authenticated the Temple

In the previous chapter we noted that Jesus was unimpressed by the spectacle of the tyrant Herod's temple. Still, Jesus made use of the temple and authenticated its validity from His infancy until the final days of His earthly ministry. Even abuses by a murderous dictator and the formalism of hypocritical Jewish leaders (Matthew 23:1-3) couldn't rob the temple of its central place in God's covenant with His people.

Jesus authenticated the temple when He was presented there as an infant (Luke 2:22-24). Scripture commanded parents to present their firstborn male children to the Lord (Exodus 13:2, 12) and to offer a sacrifice for the mother's purification (Leviticus 12:1-8). Jesus' parents did so, offering the sacrifice of the poor—two turtledoves or pigeons.

Jesus further authenticated the temple by worshiping and learning there as a child (Luke 2:41-51). Returned from His days as a young refugee in Egypt (Matthew 2:13-23), Jesus went with the multitudes to Jerusalem to observe the Passover. To his parents' chagrin, He stayed behind at the temple when they departed for their Galilean home, insisting that His obligations to His heavenly Father took precedence over His obligations to His earthly parents: "I must be in my Father's house" (v. 49). His answer is remarkable, indicating that from a very young age Jesus knew that His true Father was God, not Joseph (contrary to Mary's statement in v. 48). He was very much at home in the temple—His Father's house!

Jesus made use of the temple throughout His ministry. He regularly taught there (Luke 19:47; 20:1; 21:37-38, et al.). He sent a leper there whom He had healed (Luke 5:12-14; Leviticus 14).[52] After cleansing the temple on the day of the triumphal entry, He healed there (Matthew 21:14). As a worshiper, as a teacher, and as a healer, Jesus authenticated the Jewish temple.

Jesus Fought Abuses in the Temple

Because Jesus valued the temple as the house of God, He was zealous that it be used as God intended. For that reason, on two occasions—at the beginning and conclusion of His ministry—He *cleansed* the temple.

Jesus first cleansed the temple in John 2:13-17. Although some think of Jesus as passive and borderline effeminate, He was a man's man. And He could get ticked right off. We call it "righteous indignation" to sanctify it a bit, but make no mistake, when He saw the circus the Jews had made of the temple, Jesus was *hot!*

The Jews had turned the holiest place on earth into a bazaar. Those who came to pray—especially Gentiles, if it's true that the Jews used the court of the Gentiles to house the animals they sold—were driven out by the clutter of mer-

---

[52] Allen P. Ross ties Jesus' sending lepers to the temple to His seeking worshipers: "Leprosy had prevented this man from full communion with God in the temple, but Jesus made that communion possible by removing the effects of sin. The Father was seeking worshipers (John 4:23)—and Jesus was providing them." *Recalling the Hope of Glory,* 375.

chandise, and their prayers were drowned out by the clatter of cattle, salesmen, and bartering.

Jesus was disgusted. He crafted a makeshift whip. He sent coins and cons rolling by overturning the tables of the moneychangers. As predicted in Psalm 69:9, zeal for God's house consumed Him. The sense of ownership He felt at age twelve was very much present some twenty years later, and He defended the temple as "My Father's house" (v. 16). That's significant, as we'll see.

The second time Jesus cleansed the temple was in Matthew 21:12-17. Jesus had just been escorted into the Holy City by an adoring crowd. It was the day we refer to as "Palm Sunday." The triumphal entry (Matthew 21:1-11), a praise parade down the Mount of Olives, brought Him into the city with shouts of "Hosanna!" It was arranged by Jesus in fulfillment of Old Testament Messianic prophecies (Zechariah 9:9; Psalm 118:25-26). It was therefore another bold claim of Jesus to be the promised Messiah. And make no mistake—it was an *emotion-saturated spectacle.* The crowds *rejoiced* (Luke 19:37). The Jewish leaders *fumed,* futilely insisting that Jesus stop the praise of the multitudes (Luke 19:39-40). Jesus, for His part, *wept* over Jerusalem with what Alfred Edersheim describes as "a loud and deep lamentation."[53]

The adoring crowds looked to Jesus as the Deliverer Who they hoped would usher the Romans out of the Holy Land. They would be disappointed—and perhaps made murderously angry—for upon His entry into Jerusalem, Jesus rode not to

---

[53] Alfred Edersheim, *The Life and Times of Jesus the Messiah* (Peabody, MA: Hendrickson, 1993), 729.

the palace of Herod or Pilate. He went instead to the temple, signaling that His concerns were spiritual, not political.

He commenced with the second cleansing of the temple. *Déjà vu.* Once again we read of overturned tables and scattered livestock. But there is a very notable and poignant difference from the first cleansing of the temple three years earlier. See if you can find it:

> He said to them, "It is written, 'My house shall be called a house of prayer,' but you make it a den of robbers" (Matthew 21:13, quoting Isaiah 56:7).

Did you catch that? This time, Jesus didn't defend the temple as His Father's house, but as *His own*—"My house!" With these words, uttered on this historic day, Jesus claimed to *own* the temple. That's staggering. Once again, Jesus made an unmistakable claim to be God!

Jesus Abandoned the Temple

We've noted that Jesus referred to the temple as His Father's house (Luke 2:49 and John 2:16) and as His own house (Matthew 21:13). That makes what comes next absolutely chilling.

In Matthew 23:37-39, Jesus laments over the unbelief of Jerusalem. He desired to protect its inhabitants with the determination and tenderness of a mother hen (v. 37). Though He was willing, the Jews were not. "You would not." I can almost hear the grief in Jesus' voice. The result of the Jews' rejection of their Messiah is tragic. Read verse 38: "See, your house is left to you desolate."

Ouch. It reads like a death sentence. "Your house." Not "My Father's house." Not "My house." *Yours.*

With that harrowing statement, Jesus washed His hands of the temple at Jerusalem—and of the entire temple-based system. He was done. Although an unfortunate chapter break conceals what happens next, Matthew 24:1 tells us that "Jesus left the temple." There's something final, something ominous, about that. In a stunning display of tone deafness—or perhaps in a last ditch attempt to change Jesus' mind—the disciples chose that very moment to express their awe at the temple's opulence (v. 1b). Jesus' response was a prediction of the temple's utter ruin in AD 70:

> You see all these [buildings], do you not? Truly, I say to you, there will not be left here one stone upon another that will not be thrown down (Matthew 24:2).

The temple would stand for another 30-40 years. But God was finished with it. As the glory of God symbolically departed from the Old Testament temple in Ezekiel 10, Jesus left Herod's temple, never to return. The temple was *obsolete,* and it soon would be *desolate.*

Jesus Ultimately Replaced the Temple

When Jesus said that the hour was coming (John 4:21)—and indeed, the hour had arrived (John 4:23)—when worship would be freed from one specific location, He was claiming that *He had actually replaced the temple.* The Jerusalem temple was obsolete because the One to Whom it pointed had come.

The building was but a shadow (Hebrews 8:5; 10:1). Jesus was the real thing! Jesus is the ultimate Temple.

From my experience, Christians don't appreciate this epic truth. Jesus is the fulfillment of the Old Testament temple as surely as He is the fulfillment of the Old Testament priesthood and sacrifices. The Gospel of John hints that Jesus is the perfect Temple before John 4, but most of us have missed it.

In John 1:1-18, we have an amazing introduction to Jesus. He is the eternal Word of God—the Creator Who became a Man: "The Word became flesh and dwelt among us" (v. 14). We tend to focus on the incarnation—His "becoming flesh"—and rightly so! But what we miss is the significance of the word "dwelt." It's simple enough in English, but it's very profound in the original Greek. Very literally, the text reads, "The Word became flesh and *tabernacled* among us." The Greek word is the same root word that is used in the Septuagint (the Greek translation of the Old Testament) to describe the Old Testament tabernacle, the dwelling place of God that predated the temple.

God is omnipresent. He's everywhere. But beginning with the erection of the tabernacle, He began to *live* with His people in a uniquely attentive and observable sense (Exodus 25:8; 29:45-46).

Moses' tabernacle eventually gave way to Solomon's temple—a move from an intentionally mobile tent to a permanent structure. The significance of the temple was the same, however: God lived there. In both the tabernacle and temple, the inner chamber—the Holy of Holies—contained a mercy seat which was the very throne of Jehovah, over which the *shekinah* glory hovered.

God "moved in" to the tabernacle and temple with stunning displays of His presence (Exodus 40:34-38; 2 Chronicles 5:13-14; 7:1-3). He made Himself manifest in the tabernacle and temple. But God's *best, ultimate, perfect* manifestation of Himself is Christ—God "tabernacled" in human flesh (John 1:14)!

A chapter later, in John 2:18-22, we get an even clearer indication that Jesus would eventually replace the temple. He had just cleansed the temple the first time. Understandably, the Jewish authorities asked by what authority He did so. In our modern vernacular, they demanded, *Who do you think you are?!* They asked for a sign that would justify His seemingly presumptuous behavior.

Jesus' answer was definitely cryptic, but it makes perfect sense when you think about it. The disciples eventually understood it, but only years later (v. 22). The vague sign which Jesus offered the religious leaders was this: "Destroy this temple, and in three days I will raise it up" (v. 19).

The Jews missed it, mistakenly thinking He was referring to their pride and joy: Herod's lavish temple (v. 20; see also Matthew 26:61; 27:40). I understand their confusion. I've actually had the thought—more than once—that Jesus kind of blew that particular talk. Were I His editor, I'd have told Him to just say "body" and not "temple." That's straightforward enough: *"Kill my body, and in three days I will raise it up."* That's what He meant, after all, according to verse 21: "But he was speaking about the temple of his body."

So why didn't He just say that? For a simple reason: because He meant to say *more* than that. As shocking as it may seem in light of my Peter-like audacity in wanting to edit Jesus, what

He said was perfect and profound. I just missed it. "He was speaking about the temple of his body." In other words, He *is* the Temple!

On another occasion, in Matthew 12:1-6, Jesus claims to be "greater than the temple." It's right in front of our faces if we'd only pay attention.

Then there's Hebrews 10:19-22. I confess that I've gone into edit-the-Scriptures mode again while studying this amazing passage:

> Therefore, brothers, since we have confidence to enter the holy places by the blood of Jesus, by the new and living way that he opened for us through the curtain, that is, through his flesh, and since we have a great priest over the house of God, let us draw near with a true heart in full assurance of faith, with our hearts sprinkled clean from an evil conscience and our bodies washed with pure water.

Jesus' role as the perfect Lamb by Whose blood we can enter the holy of holies is clear in verse 19. *Check.* Jesus' role as the perfect Priest who represents us before His Father is easy to understand in verse 21. *Check.*

But verse 20 compares the temple veil to Jesus' flesh. *Ugh.* It seems like the author muddled an otherwise straightforward picture. Jesus is the *Lamb* Whose flesh was torn and Whose blood was shed. He's the *Priest* Who offers that sacrifice. Perfect. We're on a rhetorical roll. So why confuse things by connecting Jesus' flesh to the veil? Isn't His flesh analogous to the lamb rather than the veil?

Well, here's a thought: *the writer compared Jesus' flesh to the temple veil because that's exactly what the Holy Spirit Who inspired the Scriptures intended the text to say.* So not only am I presumptuous, but I'm dull! The text isn't confusing at all. It's awesome. *Jesus is the Temple!* And when Jesus' flesh was torn, the veil that separated sinners from God was torn (Matthew 27:51).

If we need yet another indication that Jesus replaced the temple, Revelation 21:22 tells us that there will be no temple in eternity. Why? Because there's no need: "And I saw no temple in the city, for its temple is the Lord God the Almighty and the Lamb."

Jesus is the perfect Temple.

What Does That Mean?

Let's close this chapter by connecting the dots from John 4 to our lives today. This is all fascinating. Truly! But what difference does it make for us two millennia later? Is this more than a lesson in history and theology? The answer is yes, absolutely. Jesus' identity as the perfect Temple is life-changing. Here's why.

The Old Testament temple served two vital purposes.

First, the temple was the place where God was *approached.* God's people could call out to Him from wherever they were. But access to God in the deepest sense went through Jerusalem and the temple. Jews were required to journey there thrice each year. Gentiles were welcome to seek Jehovah—*at the temple.*

That's why Psalm 42:1-4 has such a tone of desperation. The psalmist longed to "appear before God" (v. 2) at the temple. To be kept from Jerusalem and the temple was to be kept from the earthly presence of God. That's what made the reconstruction of the temple after the Babylonian exile so vital (Ezra and Haggai). The temple wasn't just a matter of national pride. It was where God's people *approached* Him.

But Jesus has changed all that! We don't approach God through a particular building, whether a temple or a church. We approach God through Jesus. He has given us *access*. What a blessed word that is!

> Therefore, since we have been justified by faith, we have peace with God through our Lord Jesus Christ. Through him we have also obtained *access* by faith into this grace in which we stand, and we rejoice in hope of the glory of God (Romans 5:1-2).

> For through him we both [Jews and Gentiles] have *access* in one Spirit to the Father. So then you are no longer strangers and aliens, but you are fellow citizens with the saints and members of the household of God (Ephesians 2:18-19).

> …Christ Jesus our Lord, in whom we have boldness and *access* with confidence through our faith in him (Ephesians 3:12).

We have access—*bold* and *confident* access!—to God the Father through God the Son. So Hebrews 10:19-22 concludes its comparison between Jesus and the temple veil by commanding us to "draw near" through Christ (v. 22). And Hebrews 13:15 tells us that our *praise* is received by God not because of our merit, sincerity, or form, but because our Savior gives us both access and acceptance.

Thus, John 14:6 applies to the Christian as surely as to the non-Christian: Jesus is "the Way" to the Father, without Whom we have no right to come at all. We draw near through

Christ. I love the way hymn writer William Cowper expresses this grand truth:

> *Jesus, where'er thy people meet,*
> *There they behold thy mercy-seat;*
> *Where'er they seek thee, thou art found,*
> *And ev'ry place is hallowed ground.*

God was approached through the Old Testament temple. Now God is approached through Christ, the ultimate Temple.

Second, the temple is where God was *appeased*. God could not be approached by the sinner without a blood sacrifice to atone for his iniquities (Leviticus 17:11). So the temple was a place of *death* as well as fellowship.

We underestimate what the temple experience would have been like. Artists' renderings often display a cute lamb, perhaps with but a trickle of blood staining its soft wool and the hard ground as a result of its being slain as a sacrifice.

But the sacrifice was actually a nasty, bloody affair. The animals' blood was sometimes sprinkled on objects in the temple or even on worshipers (Exodus 29:20-21; Leviticus 4:6, 17)—but at other times it was *splashed* on the altar (Exodus 24:6; 29:12, 16, 20, et al.). Imagine the scene at the Passover, when thousands and thousands of animals were slain. It would have been a gruesome thing to see—and *smell!* The temple was a reminder of God's wrath as surely as it was a reminder of God's grace. Without the shedding of blood there could be no forgiveness of sins (Hebrews 9:22).

Christ is the perfect and final appeasement of God's wrath. As we studied in chapter 4, Jesus is the propitiation for the believer's sins. It is His sacrifice—the shedding of His blood—that cleanses us from our sins (1 John 1:7; Revelation 1:5; 5:9; 7:14). We have no hope but the blood of Jesus, the crucified Lamb—offered to God by Jesus, the perfect Priest—through Jesus, the perfect Temple.

Did the Samaritan woman understand the importance of what Jesus was revealing to her? Certainly not, though she at least understood that He was the promised Messiah and her own Savior. But today we read John 4 through the lenses of the rest of the New Testament Scriptures, and we understand the seismic shift that took place at Jesus' coming.

The Old Testament tabernacle and temple were the places where God was *approached* and *appeased*. And Jesus has fulfilled both purposes, flawlessly and finally. He is the ultimate Temple where God and the sinner meet as a result of a propitiating sacrifice. Once again, I invite you to marvel at the work accomplished by our Lord Jesus Christ. God, forgive us for undervaluing such a Savior. How can we but join our hearts and voices with Philip P. Bliss and sing:

"Hallelujah! What a Savior!"

"Draw Near through Christ"

In Eden's bliss we walked with God
Unhindered by the curse.
Yet we rebelled and were expelled—
Estranged; alone; perverse.
Two mighty cherubs barred the path
To Eden's holy place;
No more could men, now stained by sin,
Behold our Maker's face.

Beneath the Law we sought the Lord
Through sacrifice and priest.
One time each year one man, in fear,
Sought God with blood of beast.
Still mighty cherubs blocked the way
So sinners could not pass—
In curtain sewn, on golden throne,
They stopped the rebel fast.

Then Christ appeared to clear the way
To God for sinful man;
Fulfilled the Law without a flaw—
Our Temple, Priest, and Lamb.
Astounded cherubs stepped aside;
Each hid his flaming sword.
With nail and thorn the Veil was torn;
Draw near through Christ the Lord!

In Jesus' name we boldly come
Before the throne of grace.
With empty hand, in Christ we stand
To seek Almighty's face
Till saints and cherubs join in awe
Around the Savior's throne.
With one great voice we will rejoice:
"All praise to Christ alone!"

"A Triune Prayer"

Blessed Father, hear our cry.
Cast out sin, but draw us nigh.
Not for merit—we have none—
For Your mercy, for Your Son.

Blessed Jesus, make our plea.
In Your name to God we flee;
Through Your blood we seek His face;
By Your priesthood claim His grace.

FIVE

Jesus Turns Sinners into Missionaries

So the woman left her water jar and went away into town and said to the people, "Come, see a man who told me all that I ever did. Can this be the Christ?" They went out of the town and were coming to him.

Many Samaritans from that town believed in him because of the woman's testimony, "He told me all that I ever did." So when the Samaritans came to him, they asked him to stay with them, and he stayed there two days. And many more believed because of his word. They said to the woman, "It is no longer because of what you said that we believe, for we have heard for ourselves, and we know that this is indeed the Savior of the world."

JOHN 4:28-30, 39-42

9

JESUS, A JAR, AND A LUNCH

JOHN 4:27-34

God clearly has decided to use the church—and only the church—as the means by which his gospel will go to the ends of the earth.

We are the plan of God, and there is no plan B.

DAVID PLATT[54]

The gospel turns sinful and thirsty Samaritan women like us into worshipers. But the story goes on. The gospel also turns us into *missionaries*. Call the Christian a worshiping evangelist or an evangelistic worshiper. However you say it, the gospel changes us.

The soul-satisfying water that Christ pours into the soul of the Christian overflows—*upward* in worship and *outward* in evangelism. As Jesus promised, the water He gave her was a bubbling spring in her soul (John 4:14). When it spilled over, she became one of the most effective evangelists of the New Testament. And she couldn't help it. As Peter said to the

---

[54] David Platt, *Radical: Taking Back Your Faith from the American Dream* (Colorado Springs, CO: Multnomah Books, 2010), 156-57.

Sanhedrin, "We cannot but speak of what we have seen and heard" (Acts 4:20). The gospel is uncontainable!

The final portion of the Samaritan woman's story contains a number of physical objects. First we'll learn some lessons from the woman's jar and the disciples' lunch. In the next chapter, we'll learn from Jesus' harvest and the Samaritan village.

A Lesson from the Woman's Jar: The Gospel is Contagious

In chapter 2, we learned that the woman was probably alone at the well on purpose. A five-time divorcee couldn't hide in a small town like Sychar, but she could at least avoid crowds. She preferred the silence of her solitude.

But her conversion changed everything! She had to share what she had learned. News as glorious as the arrival of the Messiah couldn't be hoarded. Like the four lepers in 2 Kings 7:9, her conscience bound her to share the good news she had learned. In her haste, she "left her water jar" and ran to town. She had to tell somebody—*anybody! everybody!*—about Jesus. And she couldn't let her jar get in the way.

Some interpreters make too much of the jar, supposing that it signifies her leaving behind her old way of life, or perhaps her former religious errors. I don't think it's that complicated. It's just a water jar. I'm guessing that she picked it up later. The Greek word used to describe it is the same used of the jars we read about in Jesus' water-to-wine miracle (John 2:6). I'm sure her jar didn't hold "twenty or thirty gallons" like those in John 2. But it was too cumbersome to trouble herself with it at that particular moment. So she left it behind for one simple reason:

She was so obsessed with spiritual needs that she was oblivious to physical needs.

This is worth noting. Remember, that jar had been the *only* reason she'd been there. We already know that she didn't particularly relish the trip just for the exercise (John 4:15). She saw it as repetitious drudgery, a necessity to be gotten over with. The jar *was* the mission. But something magnificent had pushed the jar right out of her mind.

A stranger—the Messiah!—had told her everything she had ever done! Her sins had been forgiven! The deep thirst of her soul had been quenched! Some news is just too good *not* to share. *"Who cares about my stupid water jar?! My neighbors need to meet Jesus like I have!"* Praise the Lord for the bold, unfiltered, downright tactless zeal of the baby Christian! As Calvin notes, "This is the nature of faith, that when we have become partakers of eternal life, we wish to bring others to share with us."[55]

Here's a thought that makes me smile: Maybe now that she knew Jesus' identity, she was actually hurrying to town in order to obey Jesus' initial command to her: "Go, call your husband, and come here" (v. 16). Wouldn't it be something if she obeyed Jesus that explicitly—*five or six times*—besides retrieving anyone else in her path?!

Whether her target was specific or general, God used her. Sinclair Ferguson tells the result of the woman's audacious

---

[55] Calvin, *Commentary on the Gospel according to John*, 167.

zeal: "One Samaritan woman was Christ's human bridge into the entire Sychar community."[56]

Among the first converts at Tri-County Bible Church, the church I planted in Madison, Ohio, was a high school senior named David. He was a starting offensive lineman on his high school football team. He was extremely disciplined. And he was crazy smart. Bioengineering smart, in fact.

Well, I met David because I was counseling his parents. Over time, the two of us formed a good friendship. I shared the gospel with him, and he listened intently. He was interested, but it always seemed like something was holding him back. I thought it was his girlfriend, but I was wrong. Maybe it was peer pressure. Nope. It was science. David knew that if he accepted Christ—if he accepted that the Bible is true—then his understanding of biology (his future career field) would have to change. His mind was spinning.

I'll never forget the day we were having lunch at the local Wendy's. He pressed me for more answers. I answered him as best I could, always endeavoring to point him back to the Bible as the ultimate authority. Suddenly, he went silent. He gazed at me with such intensity. He looked downright angry. Tears pooled in his eyes, and without as much as a word, he left me and his uneaten lunch. He was gone.

I was devastated. I feared that I had said something wrong or pushed too hard. In reality, it was evidence that the wind of the Spirit was blowing in David's life.

---

[56] Sinclair B. Ferguson, *In Christ Alone: Living the Gospel Centered Life* (Lake Mary, FL: Reformation Trust, 2007), 98-99.

The gospel seed had been planted. It was later watered by a message David heard at a Christmas concert at Grace Church of Mentor, the church that planted Tri-County Bible Church. He heard from Romans 1 that he was a sinner who deserved God's judgment. It angered him. But it stuck.

A few more months passed. David attended a worship service in which I preached a message titled "Biblical Cardiology" from Jeremiah 17:9, which describes the fatal sinfulness of every human heart. The seed was watered yet again.

Those messages on the depravity of our hearts and the just wrath of our holy God were used by the Holy Spirit to convict David of the wickedness of his own heart. As discussed in chapter 4, God used the lance of the Law to prepare a heart for the balm of the gospel. Finally, David stopped fighting. He realized he was a guilty sinner. He was grieved and ashamed. He was ready for the Good News.

David went to a local bookstore and bought his first Bible. He devoured the Scriptures. He especially focused on John 14, where he learned that Jesus Christ is the only way for sinners to have a relationship with God. After months of planting, watering, and David's own fighting, God opened his eyes. The life-giving, dark-dispelling light of the gospel shined into his heart. The miracle of 2 Corinthians 4:6 finally happened—through a conversation at Wendy's. Through sermons preached on the wickedness of sin. Through the Scriptures themselves. David repented of his own way and received the Lord Jesus Christ as his Savior!

David started growing like a weed—or like a tree growing by the rivers of water, as a friend would correct me with a smile (Psalm 1:1-3). David couldn't get enough Bible. And he couldn't tell enough people about Christ. He had no filter whatsoever. He told anyone who would listen, and some who wouldn't.

David's boldness was costly. He lost his girlfriend. His football buddies started to distance themselves. And his Uncle Joe and Grandma Falcone—Italian Catholics—were ticked right off. To my shame, I admit that I was just about ready to tell him to tone it down. Genius, right? That's just what the world needs: more silent Christians who are so tactful they are useless.

What stopped me from giving an evangelistic sedative to one of the most courageous witnesses I'd ever met? Uncle Joe did. Yes, the gospel made Joe angry. Then it made him think. Then it saved him. *Really* saved him.

A few years later, David and Uncle Joe were both deacons in our church. I love to hear them pray. They pray like Samaritan women, marveling at what Christ has done for them. But they preach like Samaritan men. David in particular is a man of the Word, with a unique gift at interpreting it with care and communicating it with passion. Today, he's training for the ministry.

What about Grandma Falcone? Let's just say that baptizing an Italian Catholic woman in her seventies has been knocked off my bucket list. And all because a brand spanking new Christian had to tell his friends and family members about Jesus, whether there seemed to be an "open door" or not.

We tend to overthink evangelism. We make it way too complicated. We teach people canned approaches that make us come off like the kid from Disney's movie *UP*:

Good afternoon. My name is Russell, and I am a Wilderness Explorer in Tribe 54, Sweat Lodge 12. Are you in need of any assistance today, sir?

We get so nervous. Our palms sweat. Our voices crack. We hope we can stay on-script. We sound artificial...and that's if we speak at all! It's no wonder people often respond to us like we're telemarketers or slick salesmen.

The Samaritan woman was anything but artificial. She was raw. She didn't know a lot. Honestly, she knew nothing but what Jesus had told her just moments before. She hadn't been to Bible college. She hadn't been through evangelism training. As far as I've been able to determine, the word "apologetics" never appears in John 4, regardless of what version you're using.

But she pointed her neighbors to Christ, and she did it *boldly*, despite her previous shame. Gone was her reticence, her avoidance of public contact, her crippling seclusion. She also gave the gospel *urgently*, leaving behind the distraction of her water jar. And she spoke the gospel *clearly*, despite her relative ignorance. She knew one thing: *People need to meet Jesus.* That's it. So she stuck with that. She was a sheepdog for the Good Shepherd. She found people and pointed them to Jesus.

And you know what? Jesus sealed the deal! If we would just give people the chance to hear about Jesus for themselves, they would never be the same.

Don't be nervous. Be so consumed with gospel truth and gospel joy that you talk about it naturally, even if a bit brashly. Tell people. Write notes to people. Share with people what the

Lord Jesus has done in your life. Invite people to church, even if you need to coax them with Sunday dinner afterwards. The point is, somehow, some way, introduce them to Jesus. It's like lighting a fuse. *Wait…wait…wait…BOOM!* The gospel is that powerful—the very power of God for salvation (Romans 1:16). And Jesus is that attractive!

Don't forget Jesus' observation to the woman back in verse 10: *"If you knew…you would ask."* She applied the same reasoning to the citizens of Sychar. *"If they knew, they'd ask for the same water Jesus gave me. And I can make sure they know!"*

The Samaritan woman sparked a revival. By the end of the chapter, an entire village had come to Christ, noting that while her testimony gained their interest, Jesus' own words saved them (v. 42).

I said earlier that the gospel is *uncontainable*. The water we've received from Christ bubbles over onto others (v. 14). But John 4 also shows us that the gospel is *contagious!* When people see a "satisfied customer"—surely an apt description of our heroine—their interest is piqued. Imagine the scene in the village:

> Are you hearing this? Are you seeing this? The lady who avoids people at all costs has suddenly become the town crier. The lady who wants us to forget about her past keeps shouting that a stranger knew all about it. She says we should meet Him. She says He might be the Messiah. I don't know what to think. She might be a nut, but I've got to see this with my own eyes!

They drop what they're doing and head out of Sychar in the direction of the well (v. 30).

This amazing story is just one scene from the great gospel narrative. What God did for this nameless woman—and *through* her—is what He longs to do again and again through people like us. What we read in John 4 should be normal, not exceptional. This is God's way.

We can see this same pattern in 2 Corinthians 5:17-6:1. It's amazingly parallel to John 4. Christ transforms those whom He has *reconciled* into *reconcilers* (vv. 18-19). Enemies of God are turned into ambassadors for Christ who speak on His behalf, *pleading* with fellow sinners to be reconciled to God by faith in Christ (v. 20)—and to do so now (6:1-2)! And don't miss how this whole process begins: God *makes* evangelists out of sinners (v. 17), and He does so through the gospel of justification (v. 21). Paul may as well be sharing the biography of the Samaritan woman!

God uses Samaritan women to tell other Samaritans about Jesus. We receive the gospel, and then we pass it on. That's how the good news spreads—not through big-name preachers, or theologians, or celebrities, but through normal Christians. I love reading about how that happened in Acts 8:1-4 as well. There we see normal Christians—*lay people,* as we sometimes call them—spreading the gospel even as the "professional" apostles stayed home in Jerusalem. God gets the gospel out through "every-member evangelism."

I keep saying that "I'm a Samaritan woman." But this time I'll back off my claim. I *want* to be a Samaritan woman. I know more about Jesus than she did. But I aspire to be as bold as her, or as blunt as my friend David. And I pray that as a result I'll come to know more Uncle Joes and Grandma Falcones!

A Lesson from the Disciples' Lunch:
Evangelism is a Delightful Duty

The disciples had some wonderful days serving the Savior. But this wasn't one of them. Their role in John 4 is to provide a "foil" against which the Samaritan woman's evangelism is all the more remarkable. In literature, a *foil* is a character whose vices provide a stark contrast to the hero's virtues. The disciples played their role all too well.

The woman set aside her jar, so obsessed with spiritual needs that she was oblivious to physical needs.

The disciples white-knuckled their lunch, so obsessed with physical needs that they were oblivious to spiritual needs.

Revival was coming to Sychar. But not because of the disciples. Remember, they had just returned from the town. Evidently, they had talked to no one. You know how that goes. You're in a neighborhood where you feel uncomfortable. You need gas, so you stop, despite your anxiety. You don't look anybody in the eye. You get what you need. You pay. You leave, as quickly as possible.

My guess is that the disciples were prejudiced. Two of them—James and John, the "sons of thunder"—wanted to call down fire from heaven to consume some Samaritans on another occasion (Luke 9:51-56). I don't know whether they could have carried out their designs. But they were so unlike Jesus!

I wonder if the villagers would have come with the disciples to meet Jesus if they had spoken up about Him. I wonder if some unexpected kindness from Jews to Samaritans might have drawn a crowd before the Samaritan woman's unexpected announcement. We'll never know. Why? Because the disciples went into the village on a mission: *to get lunch*. They didn't see people. They didn't see souls. Just a ham and rye sandwich. Well, not ham. But lunch. Sadly, their tunnel vision for the lesser mission blinded them to the larger missional opportunities all around them.

The Samaritan woman was a better evangelist on the very day of her conversion than Jesus' twelve disciples were after spending countless hours with Him. Ouch! She knew almost nothing about Jesus. They—like many of us—knew a great deal about Jesus. But she made use of her knowledge, while they buried theirs. If I'm honest, I'm more often like the disciples than the Samaritan woman.

The disciples arrived back from their jaunt into town with no Samaritans. They did bring lunch. "Mission Accomplished." Let's eat.

They were shocked—and probably a little annoyed—to see Jesus speaking to a woman, though they said nothing about it (v. 27). Kudos to Peter for that, at least. The text doesn't tell us how much of the conversation they heard. But they at least saw the woman leave Jesus and make a beeline for town. I wonder if they gave her a suspicious or disapproving glare as she walked away from their Master.

When they finally do speak to Jesus, what do they say? "Rabbi, eat" (v. 31). Perfect. I imagine some of the lunch-time chatter:

> I wonder what *that* was about. Weird. I hope nobody saw Jesus talking to that lady. Anyway, I'm glad she's finally gone. I'm starving! Where are the chips? Hey, James, pass me a soda. Andrew, you should try some of this potato salad.

But Jesus has no appetite. He treats the lunch like the woman treated her jar: *"Later, not now. I'm too busy to worry about lunch."* Jesus was distracted *from* His appetite, not *by* it.

That's the point of biblical fasting, by the way. Fasting isn't a hunger strike intended to bend God's will to your own. (Good luck with that.) It isn't meritorious; it doesn't earn a particular answer from God.

Fasting is really just *preoccupation with a great need,* like King David in 2 Samuel 12:16-23 or the exiled Jews in Esther 4:16. God's people fast because they're too burdened about something to bother with food at that moment. Sometimes it's a natural consequence of our concern, as with King David's fasting and praying as his infant son faced death. You just don't bother to eat because your attention is riveted on a great need. Other times, more often, it's an intentional *decision* to focus on spiritual matters rather than food, as with Esther— perhaps devoting your lunch hour to prayer once a week.

Try it! Quietly (Matthew 6:16-18). Fasting is still biblical, albeit out of step with the hedonism of our day (Matthew 17:19-20; Acts 13:1-3; 14:23). Were we more like our Savior in John 4, we'd be more focused on spiritual needs than physical needs. Fasting may reveal that we're making progress toward that end—or perhaps *help* us make progress.

Jesus turned the disciples' focus on food into a spiritual lesson, just as He had done with the water from the well. "I have food to eat that you do not know about" (v. 31). This is a teaching moment to Jesus. As usual.

Their attention wasn't so easily diverted from their take-out. "Has anyone brought Him something to eat" (v. 32)?

The Bible doesn't say that Jesus did a "facepalm," but I have to wonder. Mercy.

Jesus then connected the dots for them. He was focused on—He was *hungry* for—something eternal: "My food is to do the will of him who sent me and to accomplish his work" (v. 34). John's Gospel speaks of Jesus' being "sent" by the Father forty times, in 16 of 21 chapters. He is the Great Apostle (Hebrews 3:1)—which means "the *sent* One." He was sent to earth with a specific mission from His Father. That mission dominated His life.

His "meat" was doing what the Father sent Him to do (John 4:34). He was determined to carry out that mission—specifically the mission of saving the lost (1 John 4:10, 14). Though His mission required Him to go to Jerusalem and suffer infinite loss as our Substitute, He "set His face" for that city, that suffering, that crucifixion (Luke 9:51-53). Why? Because our Lord's joy came not from filling His stomach, but from pleasing His Father.

The kicker is that we've already learned that Jesus was physically worn out (v. 6). He had asked for a drink of water (v. 7). I'm sure His stomach was growling as loudly as the disciples'. But His belly was not His god (Philippians 3:19). He enjoyed food, but not nearly so much as He enjoyed pleasing His Father.

That's convicting to me, because I'm a food guy. I don't like it. I love it. My diet has been seriously limited for the last eight years due to my Celiac Disease. It's been a sanctifying experience for me. Truly.

But although I have to pass on dessert most of the time, eating gluten free basically means that I get to eat steak instead of pizza. That's my story, and I'm sticking to it. I still love food, especially meat. I'm all about "dude food"—what my family calls ribs, wings, and steak. My "three food groups" are beef, pork, and chicken. The few times I've visited a Brazilian grill like *Fogo De Chao* have almost led to ecstatic utterances. I enjoy my food! And that's fine, in its place (1 Timothy 4:3-5).

But we too easily get food and other temporal pleasures *out of* their place. We enjoy them more than we enjoy the God Who gave them (Romans 1:25). I think that's the point of Jesus' preoccupation with His Father's will, and His contrast with food, in particular. In His benevolence, God didn't make food just necessary—He made it *delicious.* It's a source of delight! But Jesus' greatest enjoyment came not from His human senses or appetites, but from doing the work of His Father—*specifically the Father's mission of seeking worshipers* (v. 24)! Speaking with a thirsty sinner was a joy, not an onerous duty. He feasted on *spiritual* delights. Lunch isn't bad. It's just not primary. It's not a priority.

Jesus had been participating in a spiritual feast. He was full. He promised to satisfy the Samaritan woman, and He Himself was satisfied in her salvation. That's the whole point of Luke 19's parables of the lost sheep, lost coin, and lost son. God *rejoices* over the repentance of sinners.

When Jesus says that seeking and saving sinners (i.e. "doing the Father's will and work," v. 34) is His *meat,* He means that evangelism is His *pleasure.* To advance the lunch analogy—the work of evangelism is *delicious!* Calvin explains:

He means not only that he esteems it very highly, but that there is nothing in which he takes greater delight, or in which he is more cheerfully or more eagerly employed.[57]

If Jesus found obeying the Father by pursuing souls to be the source of great pleasure, we should find it to be so, as well. His joy should be our joy. Richard Philips addresses this in his helpful book *Jesus the Evangelist:*

> Above all else, as Jesus shows us, our chief delight should be playing a role in the salvation of other people.[58]

How many of us get more pleasure out of a good meal than a good sermon? How many of us worry more about the condition of our neighbors' lawns than our neighbors' souls? How easy is it to talk football with our co-workers, while ignoring their need of Christ. We're like the disciples: more concerned about our lunches than the people who serve them to us. We're like Jonah: more concerned about gourds than souls.

And we're *unlike* C. T. Studd, the best known of "The Cambridge Seven," a group of Englishmen who forsook their careers to take the gospel to China in the late nineteenth century. Studd was the best cricket player in the world at that time—a celebrity—but he left his professional sports career for the sake of gospel advance.

To us, it may seem like a stunning sacrifice, analogous to Pat Tillman's choosing combat as an American soldier rather than competition as an Arizona Cardinal. But to Studd, the decision to take the gospel abroad was a no-brainer:

---

[57] Calvin, *Commentary on the Gospel according to John,* 169-70.
[58] Richard D. Phillips, *Jesus the Evangelist* (Lake Mary, FL: Reformation Trust, 2007), 161.

How could I spend the best hours of my life in working for myself and for the honor and pleasures of this world while thousands of souls are perishing every day without having heard of the Lord Jesus Christ, going down to Christless and hopeless graves?[59]

God, forgive us for allowing "the pleasures of this world" to steal our attention from those who are perishing. Forgive us for being obsessed with silly things and oblivious to the only essential thing. Help us delight in partnering with You as You seek and save the lost. Make us more like the Samaritan woman—and more like our Savior! Amen.

---

[59] John Pollock, *The Cambridge Seven* (Ross-Shire, Scotland: Christian Focus, 2009), 66-67.

"The Love of Christ"

Keeper of the withered reed,
You have wept o'er human need;
Guardian of the smold'ring flame,
You restored the blind and lame.
Move Your church to be like You—
Help us do what You would do.
Help us do what You would do.

Lifter of the leper's woe,
You have loved the poor and low;
Friend of those without a friend,
You bowed down to soothe and mend.
Move Your church to love like Christ—
Help us welcome the despised.
Help us welcome the despised.

Savior of the sinful soul,
You were pierced to make us whole;
Lamb of God Who took our place,
You were cursed to give us grace.
Move Your church with gospel truth—
Help us bring the lost to You.
Help us bring the lost to You.

"To Live or Die"

To live is Christ—I long to spend
My might and time to worship Him.
I'll give my all for Him Who died
To bring a rebel to His side.

Lord, help me use my fleeting breath
To honor You, through life or death.
And when my heart drums its last beat,
I'll lay my labors at Your feet.

To die is Christ—eternal gain,
To wake, and never sleep again.
I will not fear the feeble grave,
The pathway to my Savior's face.

To live or die—it's all the same;
For Christ consumes me, either way.
If I should live, I'll live for Him,
And if I die, I'll live again.

10

THE SAVIOR OF THE WORLD

JOHN 4:35-42

I didn't choose to be a missionary because I had counted the costs and believed it was worth it. I am a missionary because God saved me, and called me, and I have no option but to obey Him. I have no greater joy than to serve Him. I have no other passion than to please Him. I have no other plans for my life but to know Him *and to* make Him known. *Missions is the natural outflow of knowing God and realizing that we do not deserve His grace, love, and forgiveness.*

DAN ANDERSON[60]

In the fall of 2009 I asked several of my missionary heroes to tell me what it was God used to call them to the mission field. The answers I received still inspire me today. The quote that begins this chapter is from my brother Dan, who spent twelve years as a missionary in Brazil and who now serves as the Director of Brazil Gospel Fellowship Mission. I love his statement that missionary service is the normal response both to God's *commands* and to God's *grace*. Missions, like evan-

---

[60] Personal correspondence.

gelism, is motivated by a love for the Savior and a desire for others to love Him as well.

The Samaritan woman knew this instinctively, even without being taught. She forsook her jar and hurried into town to evangelize. In contrast, the disciples forsook evangelism and hurried into town for lunch. Jesus reproved them for being too easily satisfied by temporary pleasure rather than seeking the deep joy that comes from doing God's will. Now He uses yet another object lesson—one that the Apostle Paul would take up and use to describe evangelistic ministry in 1 Corinthians 3: *the harvest*.

Those who knew the Samaritan woman's reputation saw only a *harlot* when they looked at her. Jesus saw a *harvest*. He looked beyond the mess she had made of her life. He saw one whom He loved. He saw a would-be worshiper.

Although the disciples had just failed to prioritize eternal things, Christ uses the opportunity to instruct them. It's what He does. A harvest is coming, and He wants them to be part of the reaping, though they hadn't sown. He wants to train them to both sow and reap once His brief earthly ministry concludes. So He trains them. He *deputizes* them to carry out His work on His behalf in His absence.

Lift Up Your Eyes

Immediately after telling of the satisfaction He receives from doing His Father's will of seeking and making worshipers, Jesus directs the disciples' attention to the approaching harvest:

> Do you not say, "There are yet four months, then comes
> the harvest"? Look, I tell you, lift up your eyes, and see
> that the fields are white for harvest (John 4:35).

Jesus recites a proverbial saying about harvest time. To what
does Jesus refer when He urges the disciples to "lift up their
eyes"? Perhaps He is gesturing to a nearby field that will soon
be ripe enough for reaping. There were certainly fields like
that in the vicinity.

But I think the text points to something far more profound. Remember, the woman has run into town and com-
pelled her neighbors to "come and see" Jesus (v. 29). Their
immediate response was to leave town and walk toward Jesus
(v. 30). Now Jesus points to the approaching crowd and tells
His disciples to look and see the coming harvest of souls.
"Get your eyes off your lunches. Get your eyes off yourselves. Look!"

With joy, and perhaps with a hint of reproof, He tells
them that they are about to reap where another has sown
(vv. 36-39). A newborn Christian has been sowing gospel
seed in Sychar, even as Jesus' disciples have been delinquent.
But by God's grace, they can still take part in what God is
doing, and perhaps they can learn a lesson for next time and
for a productive future. *"Revival is coming, boys. In spite of you.
Get out your spiritual sickles. We've got work to do."*

The Hope of the Harvest

I can't help but be grieved by the defeatist attitude of many
Christians and Christian leaders today. I've heard men speak
as though the days of conversions and revival were past. They

speak as if the gospel's power to save sinners has waned, as if the gates of hell just might prevail, as if God is sitting on His hands.

That's blasphemy.

God is as mighty to save as ever. The gospel is still the power of God for salvation. The Spirit still grants faith and repentance. It's faithlessness and laziness to shrug as churches go months and years without seeing evangelistic fruit. My friend J. C. Ryle concurs:

> If there was more real faith on the earth, there would be less surprise felt at the conversion of souls. If Christians believed more, they would expect more, and if they understood Christ better, they would be less startled and astonished when He calls and saves the chief of sinners.[61]

The gospel is as powerful today as it ever has been. What Jesus did in Sychar He may very likely do again in our communities. Why *shouldn't* the latter half of John 4 be normal and not exceptional? Outside of Jesus' showing His omniscience by telling the lady's story, no miracles were done in Samaria. We don't read of healings, or feedings, or resurrections. Yet we still read of a great revival. We read of gospel power!

I'm so grateful for my friends Tim Keesee and Peter Hansen, who work together to produce the *Dispatches from the Front* videos, along with Tim's book by the same title.[62] Tim appears in front of the camera, while Peter hides behind it. Together they provide stunning "lift-up-your-eyes" glimpses of the most difficult mission fields in the world.

---

[61] Ryle, *Expository Thoughts*, 229.
[62] Tim Keesee, *Dispatches from the Front: Stories of Gospel Advance in the World's Difficult Places* (Wheaton, IL: Crossway, 2014). Videos are available from dispatchesfromthefront.org.

It's common for me to watch the videos through tears. I cry to see the overwhelming need. But I also shed tears of joy to see what God is doing in the world through the gospel! God is still convicting, still drawing, still saving—one soul at a time. May God use such reminders to restore our confidence in the gospel of Jesus Christ!

The Joy of the Harvest

Sowing and reaping sounds like work. Anyone who has worked on a farm for any length of time will nod in agreement. Throughout my life, I've known a number of farmers, and they're the hardest working people I know.

One such man is Johnny, a dairy farmer in Thompson, Ohio, and a fellow elder of mine when I served at Tri-County Bible Church. Johnny is old enough to be my father, and on more than one occasion he has provided me with fatherly advice. But he can still work me into the ground. Let me give two examples.

Tri-County Bible Church met in a high school auditorium for twelve years. We had a vibrant church—we just lacked a church *building*. And we were fine.

But God eventually provided a beautiful building site for us, right next to the high school. Perfect! We decided to clear the land ourselves. We sold the mature timber, but we were left with piles and piles of branches and debris. I'll never forget the workdays we had on that property. I was never trusted with a chainsaw, so I still have all my digits. But I loved feeding the chipper! Johnny and I usually took the lead of a group of twelve to fifteen men, and we worked to the point of exhaustion. Johnny was impressed that his pastor could keep up. I fooled him well. I went home and crashed; he went home and did his normal chores. But I cherish the memory of a grueling job well done.

Another time I worked with Johnny wasn't nearly so enjoyable. His wife called me requesting urgent prayer. Some of the hay they had stored in the loft of their massive barn hadn't been sufficiently dry. For weeks or even months, it fermented. Eventually, it smoldered, silently. By the time Johnny realized what was happening, it seemed to be too late.

I passed on the prayer request and then hurried to the farm. I was greeted by eight volunteer fire departments from the small towns in the area. The only solution was to pull the smoldering hay out of the loft, allowing the firemen to spray thousands of gallons of water onto the next layer of hay.

We prayed the barn itself wouldn't ignite. I joined a team below the men working in the loft, helping to gather the wet, hot hay into a trailer which took it out of the barn. We worked for hours, removing countless wagonloads of soggy, blackened, smoldering hay.

Hot water spilled onto to us from above, stinging our skin and filling our lungs with steam. The soot and stench would stick to our skin for at least a week. Noxious fumes surrounded us, occasionally forcing us outside for relief. I can't express my bewilderment at seeing firefighters lighting up cigarettes on their breaks. Go figure.

By God's grace, the fire was finally doused. We thanked the Lord together, and I returned home, looking more like a piece of charcoal than a man. I've never been so weary. I've never worked in such a frightening environment. And I've never been more satisfied in my life. Laboring with my farmer friend was exhausting—and *exhilarating!*

Farm work is wearisome, but it's a *good* tired. When Jesus speaks of the harvest in John 4:36, He speaks of both *reward* and *rejoicing.* Investing your life in sowing the gospel and reaping souls brings unparalleled difficulties. But it also brings unparalleled *delight.* That's the point of Psalm 126:5: "Those who sow in tears shall reap with shouts of joy!"

My good friend David Hosaflook answered the same question I posed to my brother Dan. How did God call him to the mission field? How might I encourage others to consider the call? His answer isn't brief, but it's beautiful, and potentially life-changing:

> Let them know the incredible difficulty of "leaving houses and lands" for the Gospel. It's easy to feel the tingly sensations of missionary surrender by listening to a well-crafted, musically-powerful missionary DVD in a climate-controlled auditorium and then hearing an impassioned sermon. But turn the A/C off when you preach the sermon. Pump in the smells of body odor and strange food and cigarette smoke. Blast some insipid Balkan or tribal music in the background.
>
> Talk about depression and loneliness and pain and smog and threats and fears and danger and discomfort and frustration about the illogical grammar. Talk about there being ten Demases that rip your heart out for every Timothy that

is faithful. Talk about pouring out blood, sweat, and tears and seeing the harvest come in slower than you thought it would.

Talk about missionary kids struggling to adjust and forever becoming "third-culture" people—neither being culturally American nor Timbuktuan. Missionary sacrifice is overwhelming. This isn't in the fine print—it's plastered all over the New Testament—but we fail to present this side because we don't want to sound like we're bellyaching. War is hell.

But let them know the incredible reward of doing all this for Christ's sake. Talk up the "joy" that was set before Christ at the cross. Talk up eternal treasure. Mention the party thrown over the 1-in-100 rescued from destruction.

Overshadow the immense difficulties of missionary sacrifice by the overwhelming rewards in eternity. Make them jealous for God's glory and tell them how incredibly amazing it is to see God turn the spiritual light on in a pagan's heart. Let them imagine how tear-jerkingly awesome it is to hear a sinner calling upon the name of the Lord, after being convicted by the Holy Spirit through someone as unworthy as them.

And even in the absence of such conversions on a large scale, let them know that there is great fulfillment in knowing that, amidst the pagan sounds and oppressive darkness, you have been sent as a light, lit by the Light. And though no one come, though no one heed, you are there, and they know you are there, and *He* knows you are there—and *He* is there with you. Always. Until it's all over and you go to your final sleep saying, "I left it all out there on the field—and it was worth it all."[63]

The Urgency of the Harvest

Tom is another farmer friend of mine. Tom was a farmer in the Midwest before the Lord called him to be a "farmer of men." He's now an almost impossibly ambitious missionary in western Africa. Tom is another missionary whom I asked to give me insight into what makes him tick as a missionary. His response makes use of lessons he learned back on the farm, and it contains the echo of Jesus' words to the disciples as He instructed them near Sychar, Samaria:

How our churches need to get a vision for evangelism! The fields are white unto harvest.

I spent many years on the farm both growing up and as an adult. Every year there was a harvest, sometimes more, sometimes less, but always a harvest. Sometimes the harvest was easy, sometimes it was difficult. Sometimes I didn't feel like getting in the combine. Sometimes I got discouraged when equipment broke down or the weather was unpleasant. Sometimes I wanted to quit early. One year I didn't finish picking corn until mid-winter when the ground finally froze hard enough to get the corn picker out there.

The point is, we always brought in the harvest. We never once left it out there.

---

[63] Personal correspondence.

Christians are responsible to bring in the harvest. The Lord Jesus has promised that when we sow, there will be reaping. The harvest must be brought in: "Say not ye, There are yet four months, and then cometh harvest? Behold, I say unto you, Lift up your eyes, and look on the fields; for they are white already to harvest" (John 4:35).[64]

Can you hear the urgency in Tom's words, mirroring the urgency in Christ's? "The harvest must be brought in." Jesus used the same analogy in Matthew 9, where He mourned over the lost condition of the multitudes and concluded with this call to prayer and call to missions:

The harvest is plentiful, but the laborers are few; therefore pray earnestly to the Lord of the harvest to send out laborers into his harvest (Matthew 9:37-38).

G. Campbell Morgan speaks pointedly of Jesus' words: "The trouble is not that the fields are not white. The trouble is that the labourers are not ready."[65]

Gospel-Centered Passivity

The modern church is all about the gospel. We read gospel-centered books, hear gospel-centered sermons, and sing gospel-centered songs, all in our gospel-centered churches. I rejoice in this emphasis. Truly.

But it troubles me that it's possible to be "gospel-centered" without ever sharing that gospel with the lost.

---

[64] Personal correspondence.
[65] Morgan, *The Gospel According to John*, 78.

If we claim to love the gospel but never communicate it to those who need it most, we're kidding ourselves. Yes, you should tell the gospel *to God* in your prayers of thanksgiving. Yes, you should remind *Christians* of the gospel. Yes, you should preach the gospel to *yourself.* But do more, not less! Tell the gospel to those who are damned, and who will stay that way apart from hearing the gospel.

John Piper shares my concern about the supposed gospel-lovers who don't actively evangelize the lost:

> If you love the cross like we sing, you must love what it was designed to do—namely, gather a people from every people group on planet earth. If you don't love that, you don't love the cross.[66]

God turns sinners into worshipers. But He also turns them into *missionaries who are seeking more worshipers!* It is a mockery to say we love God and the gospel if we don't make *His* mission *our* mission. MacArthur explains:

> The supreme way in which God chose to glorify Himself was through the redemption of sinful men, and it is through participation in that redemptive plan that believers themselves must glorify God.... Therefore the believer who desires to glorify God, who wants to honor God's supreme will and purpose, must share God's love for the lost world and share in His mission to redeem the lost to Himself. Christ came into the world that He loved and sought to win sinners to Himself for the Father's glory.

---

[66] John Piper, *How Few There Are Who Die So Hard!,* audio sermon on the life of Adoniram Judson, available at www.desiringgod.org.

As Christ's representatives, we are likewise sent into the world that He loves to bring the lost to Him and thereby bring glory and honor to God. Our mission is the same as that of the Father and of the Son.[67]

For the Sake of the Name

Worship and missions go together. We have the privilege of joining God in His pursuit of sinners who will become worshipers. 3 John 7-8 make the doxological motivation for missions clear: Missionaries go to the field "for the sake of the name."[68] Missionaries aren't motivated primarily by compassion for the lost, though that's legitimate. They are moved by a desire to see Christ exalted. They want to see His name magnified. They want to gather *more* trophies of grace, from *more* locations, resulting in *more* praise for King Jesus. They have an eye on the throne, where people from every tribe, language, people, and nation will give praise to Jesus (Revelation 5:9-10).

So again, we see that worship and evangelism aren't competitors, or even separate components of the Christian life. They're *inseparable.* They were in John 4, and they are now!

Through local evangelism and international missions, we are working with God in His pursuit of sinners. He is seeking worshipers (John 4:23) as He seeks and saves the lost (Luke 19:10). As we discussed in chapter 7, the ultimate goal of

---

[67] MacArthur, *The MacArthur New Testament Commentary: Matthew 24-28* (Chicago, IL: Moody Publishers, 1989), 331-33.

[68] I'm grateful to my friend David M. Doran for his influence on my thinking. Along with John Piper's *Let the Nations Be Glad!,* the book *For the Sake of His Name* by Doran and Pearson Johnson helped me come to understand the doxological focus of missions. Fittingly, my hymn "For the Sake of His Name" was commissioned by the student mission ministry Doran helps lead, Student Global Impact.

evangelism and missions is worship! Tom Wells expresses this powerfully, with some help from the Psalmist:

> It is not enough to aim to save men from hell. We must aim to save them for something. We must show them the majesty of our God. We cannot but long to hear them join the chorus of praise. We must say with the Psalmist: "Oh that men would praise the Lord for his goodness, and for his wonderful works to the children of men!" (Psalm 107:8, 15, 21, 31!)[69]

The Savior of the World

We've learned lessons about evangelism from a jar, a lunch, and a harvest. Let's end by looking at a village. Crowds from Sychar respond to the Samaritan woman's invitation to meet Jesus for themselves. Jesus prepares the disciples for the approaching crowds. Then what happens?

Revival.

"Many Samaritans from that town believed in him because of the woman's testimony" (John 4:39). Jesus used the most unlikely of messengers to save a multitude. He infected one thirsty sinner with the glorious gospel, and she passed on the contagious gospel to everyone in her path.

The Samaritans asked Jesus to stay with them, and He and the disciples did stay for a two-day Bible conference (v. 40). Jesus had been rejected by the Jews (vv. 1-3), but He was embraced by the Samaritans. John MacArthur explains why this was a momentous occasion:

---

[69] Wells, *A Vision for Missions*, 128.

> This passage is the first recorded instance of cross-cultural evangelism in the New Testament. It foreshadows the later spread of the gospel to the Samaritans and the Gentiles after Israel rejected salvation and the Savior (cf. Matt. 22:1-14; Luke 14:16-24).[70]

As a result of Jesus' staying in Sychar, still more Samaritans were saved (v. 41). What attracted them was the woman's surprising testimony (v. 39), but what changed their lives forever was direct contact with Christ Himself (v. 42).

I love how the record of Jesus' ministry in Sychar concludes. The Christian Samaritans exclaim that they are certain that Jesus is "indeed the Savior of the world." That's significant.

We started this study by noting the prejudice that separated Jews from Samaritans. We've noted the personal animosity, the theological debates, and the historical and cultural rivalry that kept them apart. But the Samaritans learned something that the Jews—including even Jesus' disciples—were much slower to learn. Salvation is for *everybody*. God doesn't play favorites. Salvation was "from the Jews" (v. 22), but it isn't just "*for* the Jews."

Jesus is the Savior of the world. Not just people like Nicodemus. Not just Jews. Not just men. Not just the wealthy. Not just the religious.

The same is true in the twenty-first century. Jesus is the Savior of the world. Not just Americans. Not just white people. Not just the upper class. *The world.*

Jesus crossed barriers to win a harvest, and He calls us to do the same.

---

[70] MacArthur, *The MacArthur New Testament Commentary: John 1-11,* 154.

Acts 2 and John 4

Jesus' encounter with the woman at the well changed an entire village forever. I can't wait to meet this woman—and maybe even her husbands and boyfriend—in heaven. But Jesus did more. He's the master Multi-Tasker.

He changed the disciples. This was one of many experiences that would prepare them to be "laborers" under the command of the Lord of the Harvest (Matthew 9:37-38). Although they were slow to learn, they eventually got it. The book of Acts records how they took the gospel from Jerusalem, back to Judea and Samaria, and ultimately to the whole known world (Acts 1:8). And in that great process, four great themes from John 4 are repeated in Acts 2.

First, Jesus "franchised" the temple at Pentecost. Yes, He *is* the perfect Temple, as we learned in chapter 8. But in a secondary sense, He has made His *church* the temple (1 Corinthians 3:16; 6:19; Ephesians 2:21; 1 Peter 2:5). The church is God's temple in a *derivative* sense, due to our union with Christ, the ultimate Temple. Whereas God lived in the tabernacle and temple under the Old Covenant, He took up residence *in His people* in the New Covenant, beginning in Acts 2:2.

Just as signs accompanied God's entrance into the tabernacle (Exodus 40:34-38) and temple (2 Chronicles 5:13-14; 7:1-3), similar signs accompanied the Spirit's entrance into the new temple (Acts 2:2-4)—individual Christians, over each of whom a flame of fire hovered, much as the pillar of fire did over the Old Testament tabernacle (Exodus 40:38).

The fact that the church is the new and living temple is extremely significant for our mission in the world. No longer is God's redemptive work tied to a single location. No more is the invitation given to the nations to "Come to Jerusalem." Instead, the command is given to Jesus' disciples to "Go into all the world" (Matthew 28:18-20; Mark 16:15). Starting with Acts 2, the new temple is *mobile* and ready for *export!*

Second, Jesus started to gather in a spiritual harvest at Pentecost. The Feast of Pentecost was associated with harvest (Leviticus 23:15-22; Numbers 28:26-31). It's not a coincidence that Christ chose that feast as the birthdate for His church.

Just as the disciples enjoyed a great harvest in John 4, they were used to gather in a harvest of 3000 souls in Acts 2. Jesus had ascended into heaven, but He continued His work with even greater effect through His Spirit-empowered disciples. The firstfruits of the harvest came at Pentecost, and more has been coming ever since!

Third, Jesus brought in a diverse harvest at Pentecost. The gospel didn't go out only to natives of Jerusalem. Instead, it was preached (through the gift of tongues, unlearned human languages) to people from all over the Mediterranean world (Acts 2:9-11). The locations listed are to the north, south, east, and west of Jerusalem. Why? Because Jesus is the Savior of the *world!* The inclusion of people from multiple languages on the birthdate of the church was predictive of the multi-ethnic, multi-lingual, multi-national nature of Christian missions.

Finally, Jesus turned sinners into worshipers at Pentecost. What we've observed from John 4 is repeated in Acts 2. Peter preached condemnation (Acts 2:23, 40), allowing sinners to squirm in their desperate need. The result of their deep conviction was a desperate request: "What shall we do?" (v. 37).

They were invited to respond to the gospel through faith and repentance. After that?

They *worshiped* (vv. 41-42). They were baptized. They met for corporate worship including Bible study, fellowship, breaking bread, and prayer. God turned rebels into worshipers, just like in John 4.

And then they *evangelized* (v. 47). "Day by day" more people were being saved. God turned sinners into missionaries, just like in John 4. God turned the reconciled into reconcilers, just like in 2 Corinthians 5.

As we've noted repeatedly throughout the book, John 4 is a microcosm of what God is doing in the world.

May the Lord of the Harvest so stir us that our eyes are finally diverted from the empty things that so often consume our attention. Might He help us lift our eyes so that we see the ripe fields all around us.

The crowd at the ballgame is ripe for harvest. The commuters in the annoying traffic jam are ripe for harvest. The waitress whose lack of attention irritates you is ripe for harvest. Your co-workers, family members, and neighbors are ripe for harvest. You're surrounded by fellow Samaritan women who are confused, lost, and desperately thirsty.

Each one of them will live forever—somewhere.

Be the voice that tells them how they can live forever in the glorious presence of the Lord Jesus Christ, the Savior of the world.

"Lift up your eyes."

"For the Sake of His Name"

Go to the world for the sake of His name;
To every nation His glory proclaim.
Pray that the Spirit wise
Will open darkened eyes,
Granting new life to display Jesus' fame.

In Jesus' power, preach Christ to the lost;
For Jesus' glory, count all else but loss.
Gather from every place
Trophies of sov'reign grace.
Lest life be wasted, exalt Jesus' cross.

Love the unloved for the sake of His name;
Like Christ, befriend those whose heads hang in shame.
Jesus did not condemn,
But was condemned for them.
Trust gospel pow'r, for we once were the same.

Rescue the lost for the sake of His name;
As Christ commands, snatch them out of the flame.
Tell that when Jesus died
God's wrath was satisfied.
Urge them to flee to the Lamb Who was slain.

Look to the Throne for the sake of His name;
Think of the throng who will share in His reign.
Some for whose souls we pray
Will share our joy that day,
Joining our song for the sake of His name!

CONCLUSION

There are no sins so dark that they cannot be washed clean by His atoning blood. There is no rebel so outcast before God that he will not be received through God's own Son. It is Jesus' passion—the food that consumes His heart—to do God's work of salvation for everyone in the world who will come. Let us not fail to receive the Savior of the world as our own Savior, that we might then enter into His harvest of eternal life. And let us not fail to tell the world.

RICHARD PHILLIPS[71]

The beautiful drama of John 4 has several different scenes, but it has one grand theme: *God is seeking, saving, and satisfying sinners so that they might worship Him and join Him in His grace-giving, glory-gaining pursuit of sinners.*

Jesus, the Great Missionary, is *seeking* worshipers. He is *making* worshipers out of Samaritan women. And He is inviting us to *join Him* in His great missionary work. It all goes together. Richard Baxter, the exemplary pastor of the 17th century, shows the synergy between evangelism and worship:

> [God's] glorifying himself and the saving of his people are not two decrees with God, but one decree, to glorify his mercy in their salvation.[72]

---

[71] Phillips, *Jesus the Evangelist*, 166.
[72] Richard Baxter, *The Saints' Everlasting Rest*, quoted by John Piper in *Desiring God* (Sisters, OR: Multnomah: 2003), 12.

I pray that God will use these truths to move you to faith if you don't yet know Christ.

I pray that God will use these truths to move you to worship if you do know Christ, and to evangelism and missions as the passion of your life. He's still doing those things in me.

Because I am a Samaritan woman.

BIBLIOGRAPHY

Augustine, *Confessions.*

Bailey, Kenneth E. *Jesus Through Middle Eastern Eyes.* Downers Grove, IL: InterVarsity Press Academic, 2008.

Barrett, Michael P. V. *The Beauty of Holiness.* Greenville, SC: Ambassador-Emerald International, 2006.

————. *Complete in Him.* Greenville, SC: Ambassador-Emerald International, 2000.

Bridges, Jerry. *The Gospel for Real Life.* Colorado Springs, CO: NavPress, 2003.

Bruce, A. B. *The Training of the Twelve.* Grand Rapids, MI: Kregel, 1988.

Calvin, John. *Commentary on the Gospel according to John.* Vol. 1. Grand Rapids, MI: Baker Books, 1999.

Crowley, J. D. "Check It Off the List." In *Gospel Meditations for Missions,* edited by Chris Anderson. churchworksmedia.com, 2011.

Doran, David and Pearson Johnson. *For the Sake of His Name.* Allen Park, MI: Student Global Impact, 2002.

Duncan, J. Ligon. "Does God Care How We Worship?" In *Give Praise to God,* edited by Philip Graham Ryken, Derek W. H. Thomas, and J. Ligon Duncan. Phillipsburg, NJ: Presbyterian & Reformed, 2003.

Edersheim, Alfred. *The Life and Times of Jesus the Messiah.* Peabody, MA: Hendrickson, 1993.

Ewing, W. "Samaritans." In *The International Bible Encyclopedia.* Vol. 4. Peabody, MA: Hendrickson, 1994.

Ferguson, Sinclair B. *In Christ Alone: Living the Gospel Centered Life.* Lake Mary, FL: Reformation Trust, 2007.

Gire, Ken. *Intimate Moments with the Savior.* Grand Rapids, MI: Zondervan, 1989.

Henry, Matthew. *Matthew Henry's Commentary on the Whole Bible.* Peabody, MA: Hendrickson, 1995.

Ironside, H. A. *Illustrations of Bible Truth.* n.p.: Solid Christian Books, 2014.

Josephus, Flavius. *Antiquities.*

Kaiser, Walter C. *Toward an Old Testament Theology.* Grand Rapids, MI: Zondervan, 1978.

Keesee, Tim. *Dispatches from the Front: Stories of Gospel Advance in the World's Difficult Places.* Wheaton, IL: Crossway, 2014.

———. *Dispatches from the Front* videos. Available from dispatchesfromthefront.org.

MacArthur, John. *The MacArthur New Testament Commentary: John 1-11.* Chicago, IL: Moody, 2006.

———. *The MacArthur New Testament Commentary: Matthew 24-28.* Chicago, IL: Moody, 2006.

Morgan, G. Campbell. *The Gospel According to John.* Grand Rapids, MI: Fleming Revell, 1992.

Murray, Iain H. *Revival and Revivalism.* Carlisle, PA: Banner of Truth, 1994.

Murray, John. *The Atonement.* Philadelphia, PA: Presbyterian & Reformed, 1962.

The Neumann Press Book of Verse. Charlotte, NC: Neumann Press, 1988.

Packer, J. I. *Knowing God.* Downers Grove, IL: InterVarsity Press, 1993.

Phillips, Richard D. *Jesus the Evangelist.* Lake Mary, FL: Reformation Trust, 2007.

Piper, John. *Desiring God.* Sisters, OR: Multnomah, 2003.

———. "How Few There Are Who Die So Hard!" Audio sermon on the life of Adoniram Judson. www.desiringgod.org.

———. *Let the Nations Be Glad! The Supremacy of God in Missions.* Grand Rapids, MI: Baker Academic, 2010.

Platt, David. *Radical: Taking Back Your Faith from the American Dream.* Colorado Springs, CO: Multnomah, 2010.

Pollock, John. *The Cambridge Seven.* Ross-shire, Scotland: Christian Focus, 2009.

Ross, Allen P. *Recalling the Hope of Glory.* Grand Rapids, MI: Kregel, 2006.

Russell, Eric. *J. C. Ryle: The Man of Granite with the Heart of a Child.* Ross-shire, Scotland: Christian Focus, 2008.

Ryle, J. C. *Expository Thoughts on the Gospels.* Vol. 3. Grand Rapids, MI: Baker Books, 2007.

Sproul, R. C. *The Truth of the Cross.* Lake Mary, FL: Reformed Trust, 2007.

Spurgeon, Charles Haddon. "The Glory of Christ—Beheld!" In *Metropolitan Tabernacle Pulpit.* Vol. 7. AGES Software, 1997.

Swindoll, Charles R. *Living on the Ragged Edge.* Dallas, TX: Word, 1985.

Tozer, A. W. *Whatever Happened to Worship? A Call to True Worship.* Edited by Gerald B. Smith. Camp Hill, PA: Christian Publications, 1985.

Trueman, Carl. "Compassion for the Unclean." In *Gospel Meditations for Prayer,* edited by Chris Anderson. churchworksmedia.com, 2013.

Warfield, Benjamin Breckinridge. *The Works of Benjamin B. Warfield.* Vol. 3, *Christology and Criticism.* Grand Rapids, MI: Baker Books, 2003.

Wells, Tom. *A Vision for Missions.* Carlisle, PA: Banner of Truth, 2003.

Wilson, R. Dick. "Sanballat." In *The International Bible Encyclopedia.* Vol. 4. Peabody, MA: Hendrickson, 1994.

THE *Gospel Meditations*
DEVOTIONAL SERIES

Each *Gospel Meditations* book contains thirty-one devotionals that unpack a passage of Scripture and apply it to everyday life, encouraging Christians to "let the Gospel affect their lives."

Contributing authors:

Chris Anderson, Joe Tyrpak, Tim Keesee, JD Crowley, David Hosaflook, Carl Trueman, and Dave Doran

"Gospel-saturated insights designed for the likes of you and me."
Derek Thomas—Professor, Reformed Theological Seminary

"We have come to expect meaty, edifying, superbly-written devotional entries from Chris Anderson and his team. Here are thirty-one more, and they don't disappoint."
Phil Johnson—Executive Director, Grace to You

Available from **churchworksmedia.com**.
Look for quantity discounts.

32958127R00124